Steps to Success

Steps to Success

What Successful Principals Do Every Day

Angus S. Mungal and Richard D. Sorenson

ROWMAN & LITTLEFIELD
Lanham • Boulder • New York • London

Published by Rowman & Littlefield
An imprint of The Rowman & Littlefield Publishing Group, Inc.
4501 Forbes Boulevard, Suite 200, Lanham, Maryland 20706
www.rowman.com

6 Tinworth Street, London SE11 5AL, United Kingdom

Copyright © 2020 by Angus S. Mungal and Richard D. Sorenson

All rights reserved. No part of this book may be reproduced in any form or by any electronic or mechanical means, including information storage and retrieval systems, without written permission from the publisher, except by a reviewer who may quote passages in a review.

British Library Cataloguing in Publication Information Available

Library of Congress Cataloging-in-Publication Data

Library of Congress Control Number: 2019953844

ISBN: 978-1-4758-5337-7 (cloth)
ISBN: 978-1-4758-5338-4 (pbk.)
ISBN: 978-1-4758-5339-1 (electronic)

Contents

List of Tables ix

Acknowledgments xi

Introduction 1

1 Daily Step #1—Embrace the Day, Embrace the Leadership Role 5
   Where Have You Been; Where Are You Going? 5
   Yes, It's a Journey! 6
   Who Are You? Who Do You Want to Be? Where Do
      You Want to Go? 7
   A Time to Think, a Time to Reflect: A Brief Leadership Model
      for Embracing the Day, Embracing the
      Leadership Role 8
   Mastering a Set of Essential Leadership Skills to Embrace
      Daily Challenges 9
   Embrace Involved Service 11
   Final Thoughts 16
   Discussion Questions 16
   Case Study Application—Chasing Lions:
      Embracing Involved Service 17

2 Daily Step #2—Be Organized and Prepared 21
   Getting Organized and Staying Organized—A Daily Process 21
   Areas of Relevant Leadership Preparedness 26
   Behaviors of the Organized and Prepared Principal:
      A Leadership Assessment 29
   Eat the Frog: A Brief Leadership Model for Being Both
      Organized and Prepared 30

	Final Thoughts	31
	Discussion Questions	32
	Case Study Application—Prepared and Organized: One Principal's Journey	33
3	Daily Step #3—Lead, Delegate, but Never Dump!	37
	What Kind of Leader Do You Want to Be?	37
	The Situational Principal	38
	Shared Leadership	39
	Supporting Novice Faculty	40
	Investing in New and Experienced Faculty	41
	In with the New, Out with the Old: A Principal Conundrum?	42
	Delegating: A Mentoring Act, Not a Dumping Act	43
	Connecting to Students	44
	From New Principals to Successful Principals	45
	Encouragement, Inspiration, and Motivation	45
	Trust but Verify	47
	Final Thoughts	47
	Discussion Questions	48
	Case Study Application—"And I Wanted to Be a School Principal!"	49
4	Daily Step #4—Anticipate, Adjust, and Learn	53
	Anticipating the Work Day and Work Week	53
	Checking the Pulse	54
	Mindfulness	55
	Culture, Goals, and Honesty: Principal Guides to Better Anticipating, Adjusting, and Learning	56
	Adjusting for Everyday Events	58
	Handling Crises	60
	Mindful of "Top-Down" Dictates and Demands: Principals on the "Frontline"	63
	Understanding Similar Events May Have Different Outcomes	63
	Final Thoughts	64
	Discussion Questions	65
	Case Study Application—Strangers, a True Story of Principal Leadership: Anticipating, Adapting, Adjusting, and Learning!	66
	Afterthought	69
5	Daily Step #5—Recognize, Understand, and Embrace Diversity	71
	What Do You Bring to the Table?	71
	Unconscious or Implicit Bias	72

Successful Principals and Implicit Bias	73
Addressing Bias	74
The Principalship and Marginalized Groups	76
Communication: A Key to a Successful Principalship	77
Juan's Story: "Yo Hablo Español?"	79
Successful Principals Encourage Alternative Views and Embrace Opposing Views	80
Never "No" but "Let's Arrange to Meet"	81
Successful Principals Embrace Diverse Personalities and Perspectives	82
How to Work with Difficult Teachers	83
Final Thoughts	85
Discussion Questions	86
Case Study Application—What Are You Doing or What Should You Be Doing?	87

6 Daily Step #6—Meet, Greet, and Engage in Good Humor — 89

Do This First, Every Day—Smile!	89
Do This Next, Every Day—Meet and Greet!	90
The People-Centered Principal	91
People Skills: An Essential Leadership Element—What Principals Must Do Daily to Lead and Succeed	91
Bet They Got a Kick Out of That! A Brief Leadership Model for Effectively Incorporating Interpersonal Communication Skills	92
The Good Humor Man (Woman) Sells More Than Ice Cream!	94
Final Thoughts	98
Discussion Questions	98
Case Study Application—Test Your People Skills	99

7 Daily Step #7—Build Capacity — 103

Building Capacity in Education	103
Successful Principals Build Capacity for Everyone's Achievement, Every Day	105
A Fine-Tuning Is Required: A Brief Leadership Model for Building Teacher Capacity	106
Capacity-Building and Sustainability	112
Final Thoughts	113
Discussion Questions	114
Case Study Application—Canadian Geese: An Educational Leadership Allegory	114

8	Daily Step #8—Self-Reflect, Understand the Power and Problems with Social Networking, Protect Against Cyberbullying, and Establish Professional Networks	117
	Being There	117
	Confidence vs. Ego	118
	Self-Reflection	118
	Tomorrow Is Another Day	120
	Equality and Equity	121
	In the Era of Social Media and Social Networking	122
	Social Networking and Cyberbullying	123
	Bullying and Cyberbullying Prevention	124
	Informal and Formal Networks	125
	Social Movements and Critical Thinking	126
	Alternative Teachers with Alternative Training	128
	Leadership in a Changing World	128
	Final Thoughts	129
	Discussion Questions	130
	Case Study Application—Cyberstalked	131
References		135
Index		143
About the Authors		153

List of Tables

Table 1.1	Successful Leader Characteristics	7
Table 2.1	Personality Traits to Absolutely Avoid as a School Principal	28
Table 3.1	Leadership Styles	38
Table 4.1	Mindfulness: Characteristics and Explanations	56
Table 4.2	A Step-by-Step Violence Prevention Plan	61
Table 4.3	The Other Perspective: Students and Arrest/Referral Statistics	65
Table 5.1	Types of Bias	73

Acknowledgments

I would like to thank my friends and mentors, Dr. Gary Anderson and Dr. Kathryn Herr. Gary for his patience and support, and his use of exclamation points to keep me critical!!! Kathryn for her sage advice and discussions on mental health.

I would also like to thank Dr. James Fraser at NYU, Dr. James Ryan at OISE/University of Toronto, Dr. Robert Donmoyer at University of San Diego, and Dr. Janelle Scott at University of California, Berkeley. All of whom have pushed me at crucial times. A special thank you to colleagues in my department and college, and specifically the professor's emeriti—Arturo and Don.

I am gratefully indebted to my co-author and professor emeritus Richard Sorenson for inviting me on this journey. Rick, you have been an incredible mentor through this writing process. I can never thank you enough for your wisdom and kindness.

I am grateful to my wonderful group of graduate students whose conversations contributed to my thinking. To my students who have graduated, I am very proud of your accomplishments.

I would like to thank my family (Vanessa, Baya) and friends. Thank you to my parents (Merle and Rudy) for instilling curiosity and a sense of adventure that has taken me around the world.

To the City of El Paso which has shown resilience and compassion in the wake of tragedy on August 3rd, 2019—#elpasostrong.

asm

This book and much of my work in education is the result of so many individuals who have impacted my life and career. Far too many to list here. However, I would be most remiss if I did not acknowledge my wife, Donna, the love of my life, my best friend, the mother of our two adult children, and my partner in marriage for 43 years and still going. Thank you, Donna, for helping me be a better me!

Additionally, I would like to acknowledge four important professors who helped forge in me the makings of a better school leader—Dr. Ray Cross, Dr. Buckley Qualls, Dr. Jim Walter, and Dr. Jane Wilhour. Seldom does an instructional day go by that I do not think of each of you. I am most indebted!

Finally, God bless the amazing, caring, and generous citizens of El Paso! To those who tragically died on August 3, 2019, *Vaya con Dios!*

rds

Introduction

"I try not to have ideas. They lead to complications!" —Dr. Johnny Fever, Radio DJ

(*WKRP in Cincinnati*, 1978)

Daily, successful principals are leaders who take steps to garner and share great ideas, and who assemble teams that bring great ideas to life. In the introductory quote, was Dr. Johnny Fever, the quirky *WKRP in Cincinnati* classic television show character, comical? Yes. Was he right? No! Great ideas never create complications; they generate solutions—successful resolutions, clarifications, and answers to problems plaguing a learning community!

Successful principals are visionary leaders who possess great ideas. These school leaders are honest, moral, and ethical. These exceptional principals delegate (never dump). They communicate, create, motivate, and exhibit confidence and commitment.

Successful principals focus on quality, learn from others, make appropriate and effective decisions, solve problems, establish goals, develop highly competent teams, focus on students, inspire excellence, lead openly, honestly, and with transparency, and boost academic achievement. Most important, successful principals complete eight essential every-day steps to best guide a teaching and learning organization.

Welcome to the text, *Steps to Success: What Successful Principals Do Every Day*. This book is purposefully written for practicing and aspiring public and private school administrators who desire—on a daily basis—to gain relevant skills, specialized knowledge, and overall expertise associated with being a successful school principal.

To ensure the book's effectiveness as a desk resource or as a principal preparation course text, it is organized into brief, single-topic-focused chapters. The *Steps to Success: What Successful Principals Do Every Day* is not designed as an exhaustive study on school leadership. Conversely, the text is intended to serve as an "essential necessity," providing current and prospective principal readers with relevant and practical applications as related to key daily "steps" a school administrator must master to ensure leadership success.

Each chapter begins with an appropriate quote and includes relevant experiential learning activities.

Chapter 1, *Daily Step #1—Embrace the Day, Embrace the Leadership Role*, examines how successful principals, as involved servants and transformational/high-leverage leaders, daily diagnose multiple data points, create a unified school vision, and collaborate with all members of the learning community. A review of how successful principals provide essential instructional guidance, develop an open culture and positive climate, engage and interact with students, and actively lead professional development is at the heart of the chapter.

Chapter 2, *Daily Step #2—Be Organized and Prepared*, explores how successful principals daily organize themselves and, thus, are more productive. Successful principals develop a "do-it-now" mentality, seek digital tools to augment order, productivity, and increase student and personal success. The best principals are daily prepared to accept feedback, exude respect, mentor others, communicate effectively, and are visionary, creative, innovative, and student-centered.

Chapter 3, *Daily Step #3—Lead, Delegate, but Never Dump!* considers differing types of leadership skills and their impact on the school leadership role and how a principal must daily interact with members of the learning community. An examination of differing leadership styles is the initial focus of the chapter with a more detailed perspective of situational leadership as well as shared leadership. The chapter also discloses how essential it is for a principal to support novice faculty, along with the critical aspect of investing in both new and experienced faculty. Finally, the chapter reveals how successful principals daily encourage, inspire, and motivate all members of the learning community.

Chapter 4, *Daily Step #4—Anticipate, Adjust, and Learn*, reveals how essential it is for principals to anticipate the work day and work week. Daily, successful principals check the pulse of the learning community, always mindful of certain characteristics that inform a principal as to how potential problems can occur and how to best adjust to and learn from every daily circumstance. The chapter also examines how successful principals work to prevent and handle crises as they daily and actively engage along the frontline of school leadership.

Chapter 5, *Daily Step #5—Recognize, Understand, and Embrace Diversity*, investigates the critical importance of school principals being able to daily recognize, understand, and embrace school diversity. Successful principals are always aware of and daily focus on unconscious or implicit bias, recognizing the differing types of bias, and regularly working with marginalized groups to ensure their overall success.

Communication, a key to a principal's daily success, is examined through the lens of 10 effective communication strategies. The chapter also details how successful principals encourage alternative views and are receptive to embracing opposing perspectives. The most successful principals embrace diverse personalities and understand how essential it is to work with difficult teachers.

Chapter 6, *Daily Step #6—Meet, Greet, and Engage in Good Humor*, acknowledges what successful principals do every day—smile, meet, greet, and engage in good humor. Successful principals are people-persons, possessing outstanding people-leader skills. These school leaders are more apt to incorporate good humor to better handle, in a nonthreatening manner, personnel and other campus-related issues.

Chapter 7, *Daily Step #7—Build Capacity*, recognizes that successful principals understand the true meaning of the term *capacity*. These principals understand that building capacity relates to instructionally-oriented and -directed efforts to improve leading, teaching, and learning skills, abilities, aptitude, and expertise. Successful principals incorporate, on a daily basis, a series of capacity-building tools and lead with veracity, tenacity, and perseverance.

Chapter 8, *Daily Step #8—Self-Reflect, Understand the Power and Problems with Social Networking, Protect Against Cyberbullying, and Establish Professional Networks*, discloses how successful principals, on a daily basis, self-reflect. These principals never permit ego to overwhelm confidence and they incorporate self-reflection as a leader tool to make better decisions and work more effectively with all members of the learning community. This chapter differentiates between the terms "equality" and "equity," defining and describing the terms relative to successful school leadership.

The chapter reveals how successful principals must also daily interact in an era of social media and social networking, realizing how both can impact—positively and negatively—students, teachers, and school leaders, as well as the learning environment. Cyberbullying is examined and methods of prevention are detailed. Additionally, successful principals daily engage within and across informal and formal networks, developing methods of building a support system to better ensure increased student achievement, organizational success, and principal career longevity. Finally, social movements, critical thinking, and minority views on leadership are topics for chapter consideration.

Each of the eight chapters, individually and collectively, serves to reveal numerous steps that successful principals accomplish every day. Therefore, *Steps to Success: What Successful Principals Do Every Day* has been written to build and benefit better, stronger, and successful school principals. These successful leaders are daily striving and always building an instructional setting for the greater good of students, personnel, families, and community members.

Enjoy the read!

Chapter 1

Daily Step #1

Embrace the Day, Embrace the Leadership Role

"When you come to a fork in the road, take it!" —Lawrence Peter "Yogi" Berra (1925–2015) American baseball player, three-time MVP, manager, and member of Major League Baseball's Hall of Fame

WHERE HAVE YOU BEEN; WHERE ARE YOU GOING?

Welcome to the school leadership role! The principalship, when embraced, offers individuals a career of freedom. In many respects, principals influence the destiny of many, which in a sense is an act of freedom, one of joy, actually an honor that few other professions come close to offering. The principalship, when embraced, advances a career of significant undertaking, as well as a career which—when it concludes—leaves an individual with a strong sense of accomplishment. Will there be anxiety? Of course! However, anything worthwhile in life comes at a cost. Leaders who devote themselves to the relentless pursuit of embracing the principalship role recognize it will require great time, effort, stamina, and sacrifice, but it is always worth the endeavor!

Recently, during a summer week, a new principal academy convened. Approximately 70 new principals were in attendance to gain insight regarding their new role—an opportunity to learn from experts in the field of school leadership, and a chance to embrace not only that day of leadership development but also a chance to embrace the leadership role.

New principal attendees were asked to seriously consider their own individual leadership journeys. The attendees were reminded how important it is to look back, to consider how the travels, trials, and tribulations toward the principalship created a personal, and possibly an inspiring course taken. Participants revealed how such personal and professional journeys were frequently a bit serpentinous, and in many instances a long and serendipitous passage.

Finally, the academy presenter asked the participants, "Where does this road trip lead next?" a good question for any individual who recognizes that the principalship journey is never ending, filled with many twists, turns, and curves. In many respects, no matter how new to the profession or how seasoned an administrator, the journey, each school day, always brings a new and different, if not challenging, beginning.

Along the way, it is always critical for new, tenured, or prospective principals to understand that there will always be obstacles, certain hazards, and perplexing risks, chances, gambles, and ventures—if not adventures—associated with embracing the day, as well as the leadership role!

Each day is distinctive, always interesting, if not—at times—frustrating. That's the nature of the principalship. It requires a daily embracing of the role. So, buckle up, plan the next move, and then, heighten the personal quest by delving into eight daily steps (chapter-by-chapter) which can successfully lead the current or prospective principal along a pathway to a most amazing professional journey!

YES, IT'S A JOURNEY!

Permit this first of eight chapters to serve as an initial GPS, a roadmap of sorts, that's intended to assist principals or prospective principals in avoiding the "potholes" of the profession, the dangerous detours along the way, the washed-out leaderless lanes, and the pervasive administrative mudslides. Then, to make the travels even more challenging, there are the ever-present professionally-inhibiting sinkholes, as well as the dangerous hitchhiker who is always plotting even more devious circumstances and cunning challenges.

Each one of the above-noted obstacles can be detrimental to a principal who is attempting to fully embrace the day, as well as the leadership role. Principals must cautiously hit the road traveling between the lines with abundant care and prudently guide this excursion in an attempt to seek that ever-elusive expressway leading to a successful principalship.

That said, if principals or prospective principals recognize where they've been and think they know where they're going but it's not gotten them very far, the principals or prospective principals must seriously consider who they are and who do they really want to be. There's never been a better time to purposefully embrace the day and tenaciously embrace the school leadership role. Get ready, get set, go—and enjoy a successful trip!

WHO ARE YOU? WHO DO YOU WANT TO BE? WHERE DO YOU WANT TO GO?

Often, many if not most principals find themselves thinking, as did Yogi Berra in his infamous—if not humorously telling—introductory quote, where does one go next when coming to a fork in the road? It would not be a stretch to postulate that, daily, principals find themselves at that proverbial "fork in the road"—always contemplating exactly which lane to follow, and what option to choose, if not take. Herein lies one of the many challenges to successfully leading a school. To make such a determination, it is essential that principals or prospective principals recognize who they are and just as important, who they want to be.

An assumption is presented: Principals desire to have a reputation in which they are perceived to be effective, if not exceptional, school leaders. This notion seems reasonable. Leaders of any profession, let alone the principalship, typically desire to be recognized as being the best. Ever heard a principal state: "I prefer to be a mediocre school leader"? Granted, some principals definitely are mediocre when gauged by members of the learning community. Such is a sad commentary, but most people understand that in every profession there is good, better, and best. Unfortunately, there is also less than good; how about the opposite of good—downright bad!

So, what separates the good, better, and best principals from the bad, sorrier, and worst? Consider the following. While there is no simple recipe for effective school leadership, the very best principals daily embrace the leadership role by being a successful leader who embodies the characteristics in Table 1.1.

Table 1.1 Successful Leader Characteristics

• Intelligent	• Influential	• Respected
• Personable	• Moral	• Competent
• Aspiring	• Ethical	• Motivated
• Credible	• Sensitive	• Energetic
• Loyal	• Goal-oriented	• Trustworthy

Recognize that the listing of characteristics in Table 1.1 is not absolute. Additional leader characteristics will be examined in more detail within this chapter and in the chapters to come. What is important to understand at this initial juncture is the study of effective school leadership remains ongoing. By that, it can be said with a reasonable level of conviction that the most successful principals embrace the day and the profession by making positive site-level differences. Their effectiveness is enhanced through a greater awareness of important leadership skills and school-related factors which inevitably and constructively influence their leadership growth, development, and overall capabilities.

* * *

A TIME TO THINK, A TIME TO REFLECT: A BRIEF LEADERSHIP MODEL FOR EMBRACING THE DAY, EMBRACING THE LEADERSHIP ROLE

Dr. Catherine Tomsky, a tough, sharp-tongued principal at Robert Wiley School, rose to her leadership position from within the ranks of the Bedfordville school system. During her tenure as school leader, she embraced her leadership role, skillfully conducting all leader responsibilities. Dr. Tomsky was highly intelligent, an extrovert, aspiring, influential, goal-oriented, and highly motivated. However, due to a new state-mandated instructional initiative, her time as school leader was particularly stressful—not for Dr. Tomsky, per se, but for the faculty and staff at Robert Wiley School.

Dr. Tomsky's primary concern was implementing the new instructional initiative which created additional strain and tension for the school's faculty and staff and the campus leadership team. To complicate matters, the school secretary, a beloved lady of 22 years of service, was suddenly terminated for embezzling more than $15,000 from the campus activity account.

Dr. Tomsky immediately resigned from the principalship when details of the embezzlement scheme and other school-related problems became public. Involved or not in the embezzlement scheme, Dr. Tomsky remained silent and never addressed the issue. Neither did the Bedfordville School System's superintendent nor the human resources department. Dr. Tomsky quietly moved on and took an administrative position elsewhere.

Considering what the faculty and staff called, accurately or not, a lack of leadership as associated with Dr. Tomsky, along with the high levels of stress and confusion during the principal's tenure at Robert Wiley School, the campus interview team believed that any new principal would be an improvement.

Soon, Dr. Leo Marvin a former associate superintendent from the small upstate community of Lake Moneta, was selected as the new campus principal. The faculty and staff at Robert Wiley School had high expectations for Dr. Marvin when he was hired. Dr. Marvin was calm, yet occasionally prone to emotional outbursts. For the most part he was personable, sensitive, and fairly laid-back. Some of the teachers would eventually call him low energy.

Dr. Marvin immediately assessed the situation at the school and began to embrace the leadership role by establishing new guidelines to better ensure the state-mandated instructional initiative was followed. Dr. Marvin soon revealed his primary purpose in embracing the leadership role: Do as little as possible, and rely on assistant principals and academic coaches to maintain strict control of the new instructional initiative and its implementation.

Several months into his principalship, it became apparent that Dr. Marvin was not adhering to the established guidelines associated with the newly implemented instructional initiative. A lowering of expectations became his personal, if not professional, norm. This stressed, if not infuriated, his leadership team, and most certainly created additional unease, if not apprehension, among the faculty and staff. To further complicate matters, Dr. Marvin was frequently away from campus and he failed to maintain confidences. Moreover, he took various personnel actions based on limited, if not rumored, information.

Dr. Leo Marvin was eventually asked to resign his position as principal at Robert Wiley School. He returned to his previous upstate school district, becoming a district director of school finance.

Take Time to Think and Reflect

1. Previously in the chapter, a listing of several leader characteristics was identified and related as to how successful principals embrace each school day along with the leadership role. Think for a moment about the listing and then reflect on the ways in which the leadership skills-orientations of two Robert Wiley School principals, Dr. Catherine Tomsky and later, Dr. Leo Marvin, relate and fail to relate. Explain this connection.
2. Can a common thread or threads (pro or con) be identified as related to the two principals insofar as certain leadership characteristics are concerned? Be specific in answering.
3. Again, reflect on the listing of leadership characteristics. Which of the characteristics or traits of effective school principals could have better ensured a successful principalship for both leaders, Dr. Catherine Tomsky and Dr. Leo Marvin, individually and collectively?

Embracing the day and the school leadership role requires a principal to develop, incorporate, and master a set of essential leadership skills. What are the skills, what does the research reveal, and how can said skills prepare a principal to be successful in meeting the daily challenges of leading a school?

* * *

MASTERING A SET OF ESSENTIAL LEADERSHIP SKILLS TO EMBRACE DAILY CHALLENGES

Research has long identified leadership skills that effectively and successfully enable a school principal to not only readily embrace the school day, but also to effectively embrace the leadership role. Consider the following research-based sets of essential leadership skills that enable a principal to master the leadership position.

Marzano, Waters, and McNulty (2010) have for more than a decade revealed what works in building stronger principals, more effective schools, and better students. This team of researchers has identified 21 responsibilities and their correlations to increasing student academic achievement. The authors focus on seven of these critical 21 principal obligations. The most successful principals are daily responsible for:

- *Culture* — Fostering shared beliefs and a sense of community.
- *Discipline* — Protecting teachers and students from negative actions and behaviors that distract from teaching and learning.
- *Focus* — Establishing and maintaining clear and relevant goals.
- *Involvement* — Being directly involved in the design and implementation of curriculum, instruction, coaching, modeling, and assessment practices.
- *Relationships* — Demonstrating an awareness of and care for the personal as well as the professional aspects of campus personnel.
- *Visibility* — Exhibiting high quality contact and interactions with all members of the learning community.
- *Affirmation* — Recognizing and celebrating campus-related accomplishments and admitting, accepting, and overcoming setbacks and failures.

Each of the noted leader responsibilities aid a principal in enhancing performance by being an exceptional problem-solver, revealing a strong ability in possessing social judgment and performance (understanding employee perspectives, persuading and communicating change, and handling conflict), along with social perceptiveness (understanding how individuals will react to proposed change—knowing and acknowledging the pulse of members of the organization). The latter skill has been described by some principals as recognizing if "the troops are restless."

Principals are able to embrace the day along with the leadership role by recognizing the challenge of delving into, comprehending, and applying the research literature through the implementation of empirical student-centered best practices—such as those previously identified. Reviewing the research literature and initiating the knowledge gained is but one of the many challenges successful principals face daily and labor to surmount.

Principals who embrace a challenge are typically committing an act of connectivity which requires the leader to be more open, to be more willing to shape a situation, to engage in a challenge that other leaders might face with a high level of timidity, if not utter fear. Here's an absolute: if principals wish to improve any result and embrace any leadership challenge, an increase in, if not a change of, involvement must occur. Involved service is required!

EMBRACE INVOLVED SERVICE

Involved service has its roots in the healthcare industry where there has long been a need to increase the evidence base of involvement, including an accumulation of empirical accounts of effective involvement practices which demonstrate how medical personnel, being involved in the diagnosis and service of patients, positively influence wellness and recovery (Sorenson, 2018). Data from the health care industry has systematically recorded how the novel method of involved service can be an appropriate practice with long-term implications.

Involved service can take on the form of consultation, collaboration, facilitation, quality expectation, relevancy of practice, and overall stakeholder and organizational improvement (Arnstein, 1969). While dated, Arnstein's noted work, *A Ladder of Participation*, remains relevant today in the medical field and as such, is just as meaningful in its application to principals and other leaders in the education profession.

The objective of involved service and its potential impact on principal leadership, and education in general, is far reaching and must be acknowledged. First, a clarification of the concept of involved service is needed. In other words, what is *involved service*? Beyond this initial clarification, two key areas require investigation:

1. Essential elements as related to active and successful engagement in involved service.
2. Factors resulting from the influence of involved service.

Before moving into the key areas requiring investigation, let's define involved service.

Involved Service Defined

Involved service is a process whereby a school principal promotes the personal growth, development, and self-esteem of others through visionary actions and professional experiences and services. Involved service is a means of broadened participation and wide-ranging engagement—supporting others within the learning community, improving schools, championing students, and taking an opportunity to give back through civic and administrative responsibility.

Involved service saves resources; brings people together, uniting individuals toward a common goal; fosters empathy and self-efficacy; reduces stress at the school-site level; and makes for a healthier teaching, leading, and learning environment. Involved service permits a school principal and team to discover hidden talents, seek differing perspectives, and efficiently and effectively learn the functions and operations of schooling. Involved service allows the school leader to successfully embrace the day, the leadership role, and to make a difference.

Initiating Successful Involved Service

Effective or successful examples of involved service combine traditional school leadership responsibilities such as teacher appraisal, budgeting, personnel management, scheduling, and facilities maintenance with required instructionally-oriented change to best ensure the in-depth involvement of the lead learner—the school principal. Principals must initiate two leadership acts: 1) a reckoning; and 2) a common query.

First, the reckoning, a recognition: Change is difficult. Change means altering the status quo. The business of education alters or changes slowly—almost at a snail's pace. For the most part, educators continue to do what has always been done. Why? Again, change is difficult. Many principals and faculties prefer the comfort of the status quo. Change is never comfortable. For principals engaged in involved service, a one-word descriptor stands out: *leverage*. This term simply means that a principal, as an involved servant, is a power influencer—an informed force with clout that uses (never abuses) the power of the principalship to influence, to inspire, and to lead, guide and direct others.

Second, the common query: What's a principal, as an involved servant, to do? It doesn't take a rocket scientist to figure it out. The research, the ideas, the processes, the methods, and the techniques have been before a principal's very eyes for decades. Regretfully, some principals have simply chosen to ignore (rather than be involved in) the obvious. Far too many principals continue to focus on what has always been done, what school leaders have always observed, what they have always been told to do—manage, administer, keep the boat afloat and please, don't rock the boat!

Question: Can the status quo be changed to transform not only the principal leadership role, but also teacher instruction and most important, student learning? *Answer*: Absolutely yes! What follows is a "cram-course"—a "how-to" process, or simply put, the "CliffsNotes" ™ version by which means a principal can readily and effectively embrace involved service and bring to a school essential and effective reform.

Essential Elements of Involved Service

Returning to the first of two previously posed statements: *Essential elements as related to active and successful engagement in involved service.* An examination of 10 essential, if not critical, elements of involved service is appropriate. Successful principals follow this listing, and thus reveal how involved service must be daily embraced and implemented. The 10 essential element listing is divided into three sections—*Community*, *School*, and *Leader Philosophy*—for a more tangible, if not practical, application and appreciation. Daily, outstanding involved service principals are successful because they:

Community

1. Collaborate by including all members of the school community in decision-making processes.
2. Establish the highest of expectations for all stakeholders.
3. Engage and encourage parents to be actively involved in the schooling of students.

School

4. Provide needed resources (fiscal, material, and human) to best ensure student academic success.
5. Model principles of technology and digital practice.
6. Work hand-in-hand with faculty—coaching, designing, and implementing curriculum, instruction, and professional development.
7. Daily visit classrooms and coach, model, and teach instruction for faculty and students.

Leader Philosophy

8. Develop an overall attitude, way of thinking which values the daily reassessment of vision, mission, goals, and organizational progress.
9. Train and prepare the administrative leadership teams' viewpoint, pointing toward a more effective approach to leading, teaching, and learning, and toward the goal of improving all aspects of student achievement and organizational success.
10. Transform schooling with strategic, research-based change, and then help faculty and staff handle and overcome said change.

Each of these essential elements of involved service leads a principal or prospective principal to consider how and by what means involved service impacts school leadership, as well as student achievement, teacher efficacy, and organizational success? Finally, consider what the associated factors are that result from a principal serving as an involved servant?

Factors Resulting from Involved Service

Now, an examination of the second statement previously noted: Factors resulting from involved service must be acknowledged. Principals embracing involved service will—

Initiate high-leverage transformational approaches to leadership by:

1. Examining and analyzing multiple data points.
2. Using the data diagnoses to identify instructional gaps, holes, problematic areas and, thus, clarify priorities.
3. Establishing a vision revealing how to get from Point A to Point B, for the benefit of students. Visionary leadership is all about:
   - Being future-focused (describing to faculty the "big picture.")
   - Serving as a directional guide to forthcoming plans and strategies.
   - Being focused, clear, and specific when solving problems and making decisions.
   - Reflecting purposefully and with relevance when responding to daily challenges.
   - Ensuring personal ethical and moral values are incorporated when supporting the learning community.
   - Inspiring (motivating) faculty and staff to do great things and achieve beyond required expectations.
   - Showcasing faculty and staff identifying publicly what makes the learning community better and different.
   - Asking, daily, faculty and staff to consider the following three "envisioning" statements and one final query:
     - Our school will be . . .
     - Our teaching, leading, and learning community will be . . .
     - Our learning community will demand . . . and
     - What do you, as a member of our learning community, dream?

   Again, each of the above bulleted items are daily examples of what successful principals do to establish a campus vision.
4. Incorporating what is essential to effective instructional leadership:
   - Aligning curriculum with instruction (develop, revise, and renew curriculum).
   - Providing feedback—regularly and constructively (having those difficult conversations with teachers, students, parents, and self).
5. Developing an open school culture and positive teaching and learning environment/climate:

- Establishing a collaborative vision. Determining what is valued.
- Enhancing adult and student efficacy (effectiveness, worth, value, and ability).
- Developing strong leadership and academic coaching teams.
- Setting boundaries (behavioral expectations).
- Incorporating social-emotional teaching and learning skills.
6. Building relationships.
7. Involving families and communities.
8. Leading professional development. Principals must stop delegating (sometimes, dumping) this responsibility on an assistant principal and/or academic coach. Permit teachers to know, observe, and understand that a principal does in fact identify with curriculum and instruction—that the principals *are* the "real" leaders of campus instruction! Successful principals recognize:
   - Professional development must be campus-based, principal-led, and developed on the basis of data analyses.
   - Follow-up and follow-through on all professional development must be a common and continuous norm.
9. Engaging each student. Involving and helping students. Showing students and telling them how important they are to their principal, to their school, to their community, and to society!
10. Planning daily with teachers. If principals want better schools, principals must embrace the need to develop a strong instructional program. Successful principals are:
    - Data-driven and lead data meetings. These principals show faculty and staff how to properly analyze data, and how to lead and teach with incorporated data.
    - Instructional coaches. They understand curriculum and instruction. They speak the curricular language. These principals talk the talk, and thus, walk the walk. They also build instructional coaching and capacity (see chapter 7) into their daily schedule. These principals embrace the day and embrace the school leadership role. They are engaged and involved.
    - Planners, working collaboratively with the teachers. They guide faculty in the development of instructional/curricular/teaching units.
    - Monitors who always trust but verify and always inspect what they expect!

Every principal must understand, incorporate, and utilize each of the described involved service principles to best ensure increased student achievement, faculty attainment, leadership effectiveness, and organizational success. Embrace the day. Embrace the leadership role. Be an involved servant!

FINAL THOUGHTS

Successful principals recognize "where they've been and where they're going" relative to embracing the administrative day and the school leadership role. These principals understand that embracing the day and role is a continuous journey—one in which principals have to regularly reflect in terms of "who they are and who they want to be." Successful principals recognize the many challenges of leading and regularly seek opportunities to embrace and absorb new knowledge reflective of research-based, student-centered, best-practice professional development opportunities in order to better serve all members of the learning community.

Successful principals embrace the day and the leadership role by being intelligent, personable, approachable, credible, influential, ethical, moral, competent, and respected. These principals are successful leaders simply because they take time, daily, to think about and reflect upon how they can improve by continuously seeking and mastering a set of essential leadership skills. These skills include an understanding of school culture, being focused in pursuit of clear and relevant goals, developing strong relationships, and exhibiting high quality visibility.

Successful principals incorporate technical, human, and conceptual skills. They are hands-on, people-persons possessing visionary and strategic planning abilities. These school leaders are excellent problem-solvers, effective communicators, and can readily handle conflict. They believe collective leadership is critical to transforming schools. These principals delve into and apply key aspects of the research literature to better ensure student academic success. They also engage in data analysis, community outreach, and technology integration, and they strongly believe in the empowerment of others.

Successful principals meet the challenges of leading, notably that of being an involved servant. Embracing involved service, the very best principals are actively engaged in transformational-leverage leadership—diagnosing multiple data points, creating a school vision, collaborating with all members of the learning community, providing essential instructional leadership, developing an open culture and positive climate, engaging and supporting students, permitting a vibrant student voice, and actively leading professional development.

DISCUSSION QUESTIONS

1. The chapter opens with a question as part of the section titled "Where Have You Been; Where Are You Going?" Place yourself in the "new principal academy" and respond to that initial inquiry. Additionally, think about why the road to the principalship is such a "journey"? Explain your thoughts.

2. Turn to page 7 and consider the indicators for being a "successful" principal. Of the fifteen indicators, which four might be considered the most reflective of a "successful" school leader? Support your answer.
3. In the chapter section entitled "Mastering a Set of Essential Leadership Skills to Embrace Daily Challenges," Marzano, Water, and McNulty (2010) identify seven critical principal obligations/responsibilities essential to successfully embracing the day and the leadership role. Of the seven identified, which one could be reflective of being identified as an absolute to mastering the principalship? Explain.
4. Reflect upon the 10 essential elements of involved service. Which of the elements best relates to you, as a principal or prospective principal, and to your involved service? Explain how and why.
5. Examine the 10 instructionally-oriented factors resulting from the incorporation of involved service (see pages 14–15). Which factor do you perceive to be the most important to embracing the school leadership role? Explain.

CASE STUDY APPLICATION—
CHASING LIONS: EMBRACING INVOLVED SERVICE

Arnett Benson, principal at Cullen Place School, walked down the campus hallway and conversed with his assistant principal, Arlene Zarsky. Principal Benson shared: "My dad was a principal in the late '70s and early '80s and his involvement to me, as an instructional leader, seems so minimal, if not inconsequential, today. Quite foreign, actually. I recall talking to him a few months back and he told me his role as principal evolved around plant management, student discipline, hiring personnel, developing the Master and bell schedules, as well as teacher and room assignments, conducting an annual inventory, and preparing and managing a relatively small budget.

Get this, Arlene: Dad would tell his secretary every Thursday morning that he needed to go to the county seat. His secretary, according to Dad, believed he was going to the courthouse for weekly school business. Dad chuckled when re-telling this story. In fact, Dad was heading out to play golf at the St. Patrick Country Club! Now, Arlene, wasn't that the role of a lifetime? I'm a generation too late when it comes to service as an instructional leader!"

Arlene laughed out loud and said: "I can do you one better! My uncle was a principal in this very district and he would tell of spending the final six-weeks of school, every year, sitting behind his desk, smoking his pipe, and reading Zane Grey! He said all was relatively quiet at the end of the school year and he didn't have much to do other than sit back and relax!"

Arlene and Arnett looked at each other and exclaimed simultaneously: "Unbelievable!" Principal Benson then smiled and said with a sigh, "So much has changed in the administrative role, hasn't it, Arlene? My service as instructional leader is so very involved. At times I sense I'm completely overwhelmed but at the same moment, I know I must be an involved servant. Our students, faculty and staff, and the entire learning community have come to expect my strong involvement. What's a principal to do, Arlene?" His assistant principal looked at her leader and replied: "Keep on keeping on, Arnett. We depend on you!"

Principal and assistant principal concluded their walk and talk, stepped into the administrative offices, and recognized their short-lived conversation was over. Reality kicked in and both moved on to their next instructionally-oriented task. Another day in the life of being a school leader.

Real stories, truthful accounts. For years, principal emphasis centered upon administrative organization and structure, upon certain administrative processes, upon human relation skills, and little else. Most certainly, not upon involved service as an instructional leader! Change is inevitable. Change can be beneficial—especially when it is relevant and student-centered. Change has occurred in the principal role and all must admit, for the better. Stakeholders certainly agree. Let's return to Principal Arnett Benson and another conversation with his assistant principal, Arlene Zarsky.

Later that same afternoon, following their early morning talk, the two school leaders sat down in Arnett's office for a time of reflection and debriefing. Now, the rest of the story.

ARNETT BENSON A few years ago, looking for a quick read, I stumbled onto *In a Pit with a Lion on a Snowy Day: How to Survive and Thrive When Opportunity Roars* (2006) by Mark Batterson. The book caught my attention with an introductory story about a "lion chaser"—Benaiah—straight out of 2nd Samuel in the Old Testament. Now, don't get me wrong, Arlene. What I'm sharing with you this afternoon is not a Sunday School lesson. On the contrary, it's a leadership lesson—one about involved service.

ARLENE ZARSKY Well, go on. You've got me intrigued and I'm in no hurry. Dave is picking up the kids and he's cooking dinner tonight! I'm free as the breeze, as they say. So, don't keep me guessing. What's next!

ARNETT BENSON See, Benaiah was a brave man, a valiant leader, a heroic individual, a servant to his people, and guess what? He was very involved as a lion chaser!

Now, the story of Benaiah brings to mind a lesson in principal leadership: chasing lions is exactly what we do—all day, every day! We're involved in the service of leading, teaching, and learning—often making a difference by promoting the personal growth, development, and self-esteem of others through our visionary actions and professional experiences and services. Our efforts are exemplified when we support others within the Cullen Place community by improving our school, championing each student, and always seeking an opportunity to give back.

Simply, Arlene, we are promoting a means of broadened participation and wide-ranging engagement, bringing our learning community together—uniting folk behind a common goal, fostering empathy and self-efficacy, reducing stress here on campus, and creating a healthier place for exceptional teaching, leading, and learning. We're chasing lions, Arlene. That's what we're doing. We're making a difference!

ARLENE ZARSKY Okay, I agree and I most certainly understand your point. I've definitely bought in to the concept of involved service. However, I suspect you have something else on your mind, Arnett. Right?

ARNETT BENSON Yes, Arlene, I do. I want you to think about the last time you chased a lion. Did you catch up with the lion and what did you do when you caught the lion? See, I ask that question as I have chased many an educationally-oriented lion during the course of my career, and I quickly recognized the absolute necessity of not only catching the "lion" but doing as Benaiah did—slaying it!

ARLENE ZARSKY What? You're gruesome! Slaying who or what in education?

ARNETT BENSON Don't be morbid, Arlene! I'm not a lion hater or a slayer of anyone or anything! I use the term "slayer" symbolically. When using the word "slaying" I mean "handling" or "dealing with" or "resolving" critical leadership issues and responsibilities. I'm talking about us being successful leaders of involved service and working each day to improve upon our service, through personal and professional involvement here at Cullen Place School.

ARLENE ZARKSY Valid point. I accept your challenge. Now, what about Benaiah? Tell me what happens in this "Lion Pit" story you started earlier! Don't leave me hanging here, Arnett. I'll be thinking about the story for the rest of the evening!

ARNETT BENSON Read the book, Arlene! Now, go home. Tomorrow's another day and we've got numerous tasks ahead of us. We must be the Benaiahs of our school. Isn't it great to be a "lion chaser"—we're leaders involved in the service of our learning community. I'm glad we're not principal leaders of a previous age. My dad and your uncle may have had it easy, at least in our minds. But you know what? I embrace the leadership role and work we do today. In fact, I wouldn't change my role for theirs, any day!

Application Questions

1. What are the benefits of involved service to the Cullen Place learning community? Specifically, teachers, students, and successful principal leadership. How does it relate to embracing the day, the principal role?

2. Identify some emerging issues in your school or school system that involved service could potentially impact? How? By what means?
3. Reflect on your own school and identify specific characteristics, traits, strategies, or practices of involved service. What aspects of involved service might further enhance the instructional leadership practices at your school?
4. What facets of involved service are best utilized by school principals when it comes to the "slaying of lions, embracing the day" at the campus level? Be specific in your answer.
5. Do you know a modern-day Benaiah, a principal engaged in involved service? Explain how, and by what means. How does this involved servant embrace the day and the leadership role?

Chapter 2

Daily Step #2

Be Organized and Prepared

"Becoming organized is not about changing your personality—it's all about changing your habits!" —Anonymous

"The Five Ps: Proper preparation prevents poor performance!" —Anonymous

GETTING ORGANIZED AND STAYING ORGANIZED—A DAILY PROCESS

Nearing the conclusion of the school year, a seventh-grade social studies teacher, fairly new in his career, decided it was important that his students have an opportunity to evaluate his teaching by means of a survey which included a "comments" section. The teacher couldn't help but inwardly smile when he read one particular student comment—"You're too *damb* organized and always prepared!" The teacher then amusingly thought: "Well, at least I'm not his spelling teacher!" Later, the teacher shared the evaluative comment with his principal. The veteran principal laughed out loud and said: "One of these days, you'll make a fine principal!"

Organization and preparation are two descriptors that go hand-in-hand as a daily step toward a successful principalship. There is a strong correlation between success and failure when it comes to organization and preparation, or the lack thereof. Before proceeding too far into the chapter, recognize first that a principal can best prepare to lead—on a daily basis—by being organized. First, a couple of questions. The two questions posed relate back to the introductory quotes and provide insight as to what is to come.

1. Does a principal or prospective principal need to enhance or change certain organizing skills or habits?
2. Why does proper principal preparation prevent poor personal and professional leadership performance?

Why Being Organized Matters: Examining the Daily Benefits

Successful principals are wizards when it comes to being organized. While it is a known fact that being organized is truly second-nature to some school leaders, others have to work at the skill. One tactic to understanding why being organized matters relates to principals examining their daily habits, routines, and ultimate benefits. An organized principal will approach particular daily tasks both methodically and systematically. The benefits? A system will be in place to keep track of how everything is accomplished. For example, a prioritization of the day's most important tasks is required.

Additional reasons as to why organization matters in meeting daily school-related tasks and challenges can be identified in the following "benefits"—benefits which are the result of being organized which in turn produce successful principal leadership.

1. *Productivity is increased.* Principals who are organized save time. They never break a sweat or waste precious minutes looking for the small or even large stuff. Organized principals use their time, each day, to work on important tasks, improve their flow of communication, and actually make their team more productive by being personally engaged in leading and modeling effective teaching and learning practices.

    Successful principals utilize organizational skills to be more productive because they believe it is essential to model, train, guide, and direct teachers, students, and parents. Organized principals are engaged in high-leverage administrative strategies promoting effective teaching, leading, and learning. Organized principals are productive!
2. *Stress is reduced.* Principals experience enough stress without compounding the issue by being disorganized. Stress, as is well known, is not healthy. Stress inhibits life and productivity. As previously noted, when a principal is organized, items are seldom misplaced or lost. They are often at a principal's fingertips. Searching for a dated document? If a principal is organized, the sought-after document is readily available in a nearby computer file or hard-copy file drawer, and thus, systematically filed and under the most obvious label. Such organization is a stress reliever!
3. *Time is managed.* Organization and punctuality are tantamount to a principal's success as both go hand-in-glove with meeting deadlines, being on time, and establishing time-oriented schedules. Daily time management skills permit a principal to establish and maintain deadlines to effect

best-practice curricular and instructional requirements, develop class/teacher schedules and action plans, prioritize and assign tasks, organize daily, weekly, monthly, and yearly timelines, delegate certain supervisory and managerial tasks, and complete important projects.

An exceptional time-oriented and being organized read is *The Principal's Guide to Time Management: Instructional Leadership in the Digital Age* (2016). Finally, consider the following: Principals who are daily organized and productive become the masters of their minutes. Recognize that time is a scarce commodity and unless it is managed, nothing else can be managed.

4. *Planning and collaboration are improved.* Planning for and collaborating with members of the learning community is an absolute. Many principals need assistance with their daily organizational and preparation responsibilities. Seldom does the school-site office enjoy enough in-house employees to handle all of the administrative-oriented and organizational tasks and responsibilities.

    It is absolutely essential for a principal to recognize the need for additional office assistance. This means finding the necessary personnel to aid with the daily managerial tasks. However, funding is *always* an issue. One sure-fire method for finding these helpers is to look at who is in plain sight—parent and other volunteers. Most principals observe volunteers working in classrooms, material centers, workrooms, libraries, and computer labs. Why not seek out one or two volunteers who possess strong organizational skills and confidentiality abilities and permit them to volunteer in the campus offices—even in the principal's office. One absolute: Volunteers must never be moved from one service location to another at the expense of students.

    When an in-house organizational problem exists, plan to find a volunteer who can assist a principal and administrative team in being better organized and prepared. If funding is available, always spend the dollars wisely and prudently to best ensure the right employee (highly competent and most confidential) is hired to aid in the office area. Being daily organized better frees a principal to more effectively and efficiently collaborate instructionally with faculty, staff, students, and parents.

5. *Reputation is enhanced.* If a principal looks organized and is organized, the principal looks good and people notice. If a principal looks good (professionally), a principal feels good. An organized principal gets more done each day and is able to keep up with important matters. Faculty and staff notice. Daily, principal tasks are completed in a timely manner and, again, people notice. Requests are handled effectively and efficiently, and people notice. All administrative and managerial tasks are expediently completed, and people notice. Finally, a principal's reputation as a successful leader is enhanced and, again, people notice.

6. *Promotion possibilities increase.* Principals who have a reputation for being effectively organized, who plan efficiently and collaborate regularly, who manage their time appropriately, and who are productive, are most likely to be promoted. Organized principals are talked about, positively, by supervisors, by faculty and staff, by parents, and by other members of the learning community. That positive talk generally includes comments such as "She'll be promoted soon" or "He's a likely candidate to be promoted." A principal may not necessarily be seeking a promotion, but isn't it nice to know that other school district personnel are thinking and talking about such promotion possibilities.
7. *Obsolete, unusable, and unneeded items are reduced.* An organized principal maintains on a daily basis an organized office. An organized office is quickly rid of dated paperwork and materials, obsolete hardware and software, and even old and dilapidated furniture—all of which are typically no longer practical/serviceable/operational, and thus, nonessential. Some principals actually have a weekly "Toss-It Tuesday!" Remember, if it doesn't enhance the administrative office or serve to assist—get rid of it and get better organized.
8. *Workspace is more open, accessible, and attractive.* The best place to begin getting organized is a principal's workspace—both physical and virtual. Both are equally important to the success of a principal. If the area is messy and disorganized, a principal (as previously noted) will be stressed. So, organized principals develop a daily process of filing items—both in the file cabinet and on the virtual desktop. This daily process eliminates the misplacing of loose papers and documents, to include emails, texts, and/or other digital applications. A neat, organized workspace makes for an attractive office where people feel welcome, and where a principal looks not only capable, but successful—if not essential.
9. *Self-esteem and confidence are increased.* Reconsider Item #5—if a principal looks good and feels good, well, all is typically good. Being daily organized is an exceptional method for building self-esteem and personal confidence. A principal will feel better, mentally and emotionally, when all is in good order. Orderliness produces a positive self-esteem which correlates with increased confidence, better performance, happiness, a healthier attitude and lifestyle, along with interpersonal as well as organizational success (Baumeister, Campbell, Krueger, & Vohs, 2003). Successful principals begin each workday by striving to be more organized. Being organized permits a principal to feel better and do better.
10. *Relationships are improved.* Being organized affects more than a principal's work environment. Being organized on a daily basis, as noted in Item #9, strongly correlates with positive interpersonal relationships.

Principals who are organized develop and cultivate improved relationships with friends, family, and co-workers. Unorganized individuals are much more apt to foster frustration and resentment in others.

Being organized each day better ensures a principal will keep promises and commitments. These principals are the beneficiaries of not only being organized, they are known for being responsible, dependable, and as a result, they are appreciated. Moreover, these principals are more likely to build positive personal and professional relationships.

The Top-10 Daily Habits and Routines Essential to Becoming an Organized Principal

Organized principals run the day and therefore, do not permit the day to run them. Listed below are the Top-10 Daily Habits and Routines essential to becoming better organized in the administrative office setting, and thus, becoming more successful. Follow this listing:

1. Everything has a specific place in the principal's office.
2. Return everything to its place. That's what organized principals do.
3. Establish parameters. If something comes into the office, something must go out of the office.
4. Use items such as file drawers, desk drawers, cabinet shelves and drawers, desk drawer bins and containers, and desktop baskets as a means of keeping items organized and in their place.
5. Small organized steps equal large organizational gains. Becoming organized on a daily basis makes others perceive a principal as being highly competent.
6. Ensure that at least one area on the principal's desk is organized at all times.
7. Do the above NOW! Do what follows immediately thereafter!
8. Never leave an organizing effort or project partially completed. Take a few minutes at the beginning of each day and/or at the conclusion of each day to organize and complete unfinished tasks. By doing so, a principal will start the day and finish the day on the right note.
9. Reward yourself for all organizing efforts, large or small. The authors of this text will jump hurdles (even organize quickly) for chocolate!
10. Though clutter and disorganization will inevitably strive to prevail—don't let it! Follow the Top-10 Daily Habits and Routines, as well as all of the guidelines identified within this chapter, and a new and better organized principal will emerge!

A Dozen Daily Principal Leadership Practices

Successful principals, as already noted, are organized. They exhibit principal leadership practices which ensure faculty, staff, students, and parents recognize that the school leader is willing, able, and ready to effectively lead the entire school community. The organized principal daily incorporates the following leadership practices:

- Writes down or dictates (by hand or electronically) information, maintains a current to-do list, and offers notes of encouragement and challenge to others;
- Establishes daily habits and routines that enhance, if not ensure, organization;
- Understands the importance of where and how to ask for help;
- Exhibits optimism and creates a goal-orientation;
- Never puts off important actions, projects, or activities;
- Develops a "do-it-now" mentality and approach to leading;
- Uni-tasks. The more efficient, effective, and organized leaders attend to one task at a time. Multitasking essentially spreads attention to detail typically way too thin thus creating disorganization;
- Seeks out digital/technological tools for assuring daily instructional effectiveness and overall productivity;
- Identifies three "must-do" instructionally-oriented activities or tasks each morning as a means for promoting the start of an organized and thus, successful day;
- Creates schedules and adheres to deadlines;
- Promptly and regularly (multiple times daily) responds/replies to emails; and
- Checks and clears out all emails, texts, mobile group messaging, and other digital applications each day.

Being daily organized is a fundamental leadership practice that all principals should embrace. Being organized enhances all aspects of the leadership role. In fact, no school leader can succeed to any great degree without being organized. Being organized does not require a principal to change his or her personality; it requires certain habits and routines be enhanced. Reflect on the following Benjamin Franklin quote: "For every minute spent organizing, an hour is earned" (Google Quotes, 2019). Remember, the very best principals are organized and thus, empowered. As a result, daily, they succeed!

AREAS OF RELEVANT LEADERSHIP PREPAREDNESS

Recent and significant efforts have better defined the research-based performance capacities required of principals who must successfully lead schools in this current era of continuous improvement and accountability. Very specific core skills are critical to leading at the school-site level and are identified in the *7 Bs of Preparedness*. Daily, principals must:

1. *Be prepared* to experience and understand a wide-range of school-site demands (Cray & Wailer, 2011);
2. *Be prepared* to effectively incorporate the best teaching, coaching, leading, and learning practices (Bambrick-Santoyo, 2018; Marzano, Waters, & McNulty, 2010);
3. *Be prepared* to utilize exceptional personnel management practices and strategies (Sorenson & Goldsmith, 2009);
4. *Be prepared* to develop strong organizational skills to handle the dictates and demands of the leadership role (Whitaker, 2012);
5. *Be prepared* to appreciate the impact, emphasis, and influence of high-leverage coaching (Bambrick-Santoyo, 2018; Desravines, Aquino, & Fenton, 2016; and Fullan, 2014);
6. *Be prepared* to equitably educate all students. This is called leadership for social justice. (Brown & Shaked, 2018; and Miller & Martin, 2014); and
7. *Be prepared* to meet the challenges of instructional leadership—challenges which are ever-evolving, demanding, and frequently, quite frustrating (Northouse, 2017).

The obvious focus of these research-based skill sets, as related to successful principal leadership, is preparation and organization.

Therefore, school principals must daily enhance and develop the following characteristics or traits of leadership preparedness: Creativeness, possessing a high level of intelligence, maintaining an even temperament, being achievement-oriented, assertive, task- as well as relationship-oriented, showcasing effective communication skills, being self-confident, dependable, responsible, energetic, tolerant, adjustable, and having sociability, as well as possessing feedback skills. Principals must be prepared to daily incorporate quality-orientations, apply situational leadership influences, possess strong moral and ethical dimensions, and utilize active listening skills.

Successful Principal Preparedness Attributes

Identified are several additional principal preparedness attributes, characteristics, and/or skills that include: (1) maintaining a positive self-concept; (2) developing a high self-esteem; (3) accepting feedback; (4) being nonjudgmental, as well as nondefensive; and (5) avoiding the following personality

Table 2.1 Personality Traits to Absolutely Avoid as a School Principal

• Overbearing	• Hostile	• Egotistical
• Domineering	• Introverted	• Cynical
• Insulting	• Judgmental	• Neurotic
• Highly evaluative of others	• Unorganized (thus, undependable, irresponsible)	• Sociopathic
		• Narcissistic
• Authoritative	• Selfish	• Ultra-sensitive or emotional
• Impatient	• Indolent	
• Pessimistic		• Psychopathic
		• Machiavellianistic

traits—each of which can readily relate to inappropriate, if not unethical and/or immoral, leader behaviors. A principal showcases preparedness by *never* embodying the traits listed in Table 2.1.

Each of these particular and less than desirable personality attributes in Table 2.1 can best be described as falling into the category of ineffective and unprepared leadership, sadly suggesting that a principal who possesses any of the above noted attributes is anything but a successful leader. In other words, these principals are not prepared to lead or serve. Principals must adopt positive personality attributes and avoid those most pervasive and negative personality traits.

Principals must be daily prepared to take on positive and appropriate traits, responsibilities, characteristics, and attributes for almost any given situation. Principals must be prepared to lead by incorporating high-leverage leadership strategies. These principals:

- Provide mentorship: Exude respect and demonstrate professionalism;
- Act strategically: Understand follower-leader dynamics (professional socialization);
- Communicate effectively and regularly: Demonstrate an ability to be alert in interactions, responsive in engagements, active in visibility, and quick-thinking and level-headed in reactions and replies;
- Develop a vision for the future: Always looking at today, and in advance toward tomorrow, next week, next month, next semester, next year, and the next three- to five-years;
- Manage complexity: Exhibit self-management (they are prepared and organized);
- Create long-lasting relationships: Engage in accountability and responsibility toward self and others;
- Exhibit and foster creativity and innovation: Establish a lasting and positive legacy—one in which students, faculty, staff, parents, and community members recognize a compassionate and caring individual of integrity—certainly, a student-centered school leader.

BEHAVIORS OF THE ORGANIZED AND PREPARED PRINCIPAL: A LEADERSHIP ASSESSMENT

Identified below are several personal, people, and strategic high-leverage leadership and stakeholder-focused behaviors as related to a principal's organization skills and preparedness capabilities. Take a few minutes to complete the Likert scale listing identifying, by a measure of 1 to 5 (see an explanation below), those items that relate to your own professional life. How do you measure up? Are you exhibiting the behaviors of a prepared and organized principal? See the scoring instructions below.

1 = I strongly disagree   2 = I somewhat disagree   3 = No opinion
4 = I somewhat agree   5 = I strongly agree

I, as principal or prospective principal:

____ Demonstrate a personal and professional commitment to being effectively organized in all of my instructional leadership endeavors.

____ Prepare to work effectively with employees at all levels, actively promoting and modeling collaboration.

____ Establish an attitude of and commitment to being prepared in all circumstances and situations, including to always expect the unexpected.

____ Organize, prepare, and display extensive and effective leader communication skills.

____ Encourage others to articulate regular and open expressions of student-centered ideas and innovations.

____ Respond resourcefully, organizationally, and in a most prepared manner to change, ambiguity, and setbacks.

____ Collaboratively organize and prepare for opportunities of innovation and risk-taking, making research-based, student-centered best practices a reality.

____ Prepare to follow through on professional commitments to the learning community.

____ Organize my office, prepare effectively for faculty meetings, and organize and prepare for all other meetings to include parent meetings, Special Education meetings, and parent-teacher association meetings.

____ Prepare and organize when making decisions and solving problems—always reminding myself and others that students come first.

____ Prepare to best understand and effectively relate to comprehending instructional issues, demonstrating a passion for exceeding expectations.

____ Organize and prepare to demonstrate a commitment to be a person of integrity in all personal and professional endeavors.

____ Prepare to link strategies, priorities, people, and fiscal assets to best produce results that exceed expectations.

____ Prepare to utilize research-based information and best practices to place all members of the learning community in a competitive position to overcome challenges and to make strategic changes to better direct student and organizational achievement.

____ Finally, *Eat the frog!* Recall the quote from Mark Twain: "Eat a live frog first thing in the morning and nothing worse will happen to you the rest of the day" (Rasmussen, 1998, p. 114). In other words, complete—first and foremost—each morning the one task least desired. In doing so, a principal will have a more productive and organized day without that one distasteful task constantly weighing on the mind.

Scoring Instructions

Divide the sum of the scores by 15 for an average score.

Meaning of Score: The higher an average score, the more likely a principal or prospective principal is predisposed to exhibit the behaviors of an organized and prepared school leader.

The lower an average score, just the opposite. The more likely a principal or prospective principal is predisposed to exhibit the behaviors of an unorganized and unprepared school leader.

Again, how do you measure up? What did you learn about yourself? Are you exhibiting behaviors of a prepared and organized principal?

* * *

EAT THE FROG: A BRIEF LEADERSHIP MODEL FOR BEING BOTH ORGANIZED AND PREPARED

The *Eat the Frog* quote brings to mind the story of an organized principal, Dr. Benton C. Quest, who shared what he liked most about his role as school leader. First, this principal revealed what he really disliked—a particular administrative report that had to be completed and submitted to the district office by early Tuesday morning of each school week.

Principal Quest found the report to be a needless obligation as the required paperwork, once submitted, was quickly filed and never actually reviewed by anyone at the district offices. It was, however, nonnegotiable. Thus, Dr. Quest thought the process was simply a waste of time since he preferred to use his valuable time being out and about, positively influencing and inspiring students and teachers.

The required weekly report interfered with the principal's true love of leading—helping others work through problems, and using his time to seek instructional solutions to the numerous issues that inhibited effective teaching, leading, and learning. In fact, Dr. Quest often stated: "I love stepping into classrooms where something instructionally-focused and interesting is occurring, where students are academically challenged and engaged, and where the students are socially interactive."

Dr. Quest found great inspiration observing and interacting with students as they mastered special lessons or learning tasks, or completed course-related projects, or daily academic assignments. The faces of the students aglow in the myriad of mystery, anticipation, intrigue, and the thrill of learning excited the school leader. The principal was fond of saying: "Now, tell me, what other job gives a person all of this special responsibility?"

Principal Quest went on to share: "Why should I be required to give up those important moments with students to complete a report nobody reads? It makes no sense! But, it's a requirement. I am prepared to do it. *I eat the frog*. It's a bitter swallow, but it's the first thing I do every Tuesday morning and I do it before the school day begins. Most principals take time to complete the report during the school day on Monday. Not me!

"Here's what I do," relates Dr. Quest: "I organize my schedule, slip away from my home early Tuesday morning, and arrive at the office a few hours earlier than normal to do a task I'd rather avoid. The evening before, I ensure my desk is clear of potential distractions so I won't be consumed with something else that is either more important or more interesting. I organize myself and my office to meet the district paperwork dictate!"

Dr. Quest then added: "Because I'm prepared and I've organized completing the weekly report into my before-the-school-day-starts schedule, I don't have to dump it on Jade Kallum, my secretary, or leave it with my assistant principal, Roger Bannon. I'm free—prior to the first bell sounding—to do what I love most: I'm free to be with students. You know what? This isn't a job—it's a calling!"

* * *

FINAL THOUGHTS

Successful principals daily organize themselves and thus, are productive. They manage time effectively, plan and collaborate with others, and have impeccable reputations. Exceptionally organized principals are more likely to be promoted. These same organized principals are more apt to have an open, accessible, and attractive office—if not school, have a high self-esteem, and are confident in the work they do each day and how they lead. Exceptionally organized principals build strong relationships with others across the learning community, and they avoid leaving a partially completed organizing effort or project. These school leaders are positively and regularly noticed by others.

Successful principals lead an organized daily effort to purge office clutter, avoid putting activities and/or actions off, and have long developed a "do-it-now" philosophy. These principals seek technological (digital) tools to increase order, productivity, and to also increase student and personal success. They identify and initiate at least three "must-do" activities each day, create and adhere to daily schedules and deadlines, and regularly and promptly respond to emails.

Successful principals are always prepared to lead. They possess specific core skills that enable them to be prepared. These skills include: experiencing and understanding a wide-range of school-site demands, utilizing exceptional personnel management practices and strategies, and meeting the challenges of instructional leadership which at times are more than ever-evolving or demanding, and many of which can be frustrating.

Successful principals are daily prepared to maintain a positive self-concept and attitude, accept feedback (both positive and negative), are nonjudgmental and nondefensive, and avoid personality characteristics or traits that can at best be identified as being inappropriate, unethical and/or immoral. These best-prepared principals exude respect and demonstrate professionalism, mentor others, communicate effectively, are active listeners, visionary, creative, and innovative, and work to establish a long-lasting and positive legacy. Exceptionally prepared principals are definitely student-centered.

Finally, successful principals work to ensure that future school leaders are best suited and trained to be organized and prepared to lead in a most honorable, yet extremely demanding profession. These successful principals also *eat the frog* first, each and every day! By doing so, they can best commit to the success of all members of the learning community.

DISCUSSION QUESTIONS

1. Based on the chapter reading, provide evidence as to why it is essential for a principal or prospective principal to be organized. Consider those skills most needed to be improved upon relative to those already mastered.
2. Consider the 10 daily benefits as to why being organized matters. Of the 10 benefits, which three might be perceived to be most essential to effective principal organization and success? Provide an explanation for each answer.

3. Examine the chapter section entitled "The Top-10 Daily Habits and Routines Essential to Becoming an Organized Principal" and present a case as to which two are the *most* essential habits and/or routines for a principal or prospective principal to acquire.
4. An old anonymous saying, "Being organized is being in control," could best relate to which one of these three daily leadership practices? Explain the reasoning as associated with the chosen answer. The best organized principal:
   - Writes down or dictates information, maintaining a current to-do list; or
   - Uni-tasks. Multi tasking essentially spreads attention to detail typically way too thin.
   - Identifies three "must-do" activities or tasks each morning to start a day.
5. Prepared principals develop, enhance, and exhibit certain characteristics or traits of leadership preparedness. Examples include, but are not limited to, being creative, intelligent, assertive, communicative, energetic, adjustable or flexible, and being an active listener. Which one of these noted traits is an essential, if not critical, element of a prepared school leader? Explain.
6. Prepared principals incorporate high-leverage leadership strategies. Of the fifteen strategies listed on pages 29–30 of this chapter, which four—in priority order—do you believe must be targeted for your own professional growth and development?

CASE STUDY APPLICATION—PREPARED AND ORGANIZED: ONE PRINCIPAL'S JOURNEY

Dr. Sandra Rios stood in the common area of the school she led as principal. Students passed between classes. Many spoke or waved to their principal as they made their way to the differing hallways that housed their teachers and courses. Dr. Rios—in return—smiled, waved, and spoke to the students. She loved her role as school leader.

Dr. Rios had worked hard to earn the position. She was selected for the leadership role for numerous reasons, including her leadership skills and capacity, planning strategies, motivational abilities, and talent to monitor and correct organizational deviations. Dr. Rios was truly a leader of people, talented to the point that her superintendent earlier that day asked her the following while visiting her campus: "Sandra, how do you do it? How do you bring it all together?"

Dr. Rios could now smile as she reflected back on the superintendent's query. She had responded in a low-key but confident voice: "I manage to be both organized and prepared. But you must know that getting to this point has been a journey." As is the case with most superintendents, this one was in a hurry and shouted back to the principal as he hurriedly left the school building: "Tell me sometime. I'd like to know about your journey." Sandra at that moment laughed quietly to herself, thinking: "It wasn't always easy."

Dr. Sandra Rios had always been an outstanding educator—teacher, counselor, assistant principal, and now principal. She had worked mostly in a man's world. She had worked with several principals—one who was humorous, J. Algernon Hawthorne; one who was demanding, Gideon Auerbach; one who was simply lazy, Arthur Shelby; and one who was probably the most complete insofar as school leaders were concerned: T. G. Culpepper.

Dr. Sandra Rios had served as an assistant principal to Mr. Culpepper. He was straightforward and results-oriented, and possessed a love of teaching and leading. He was simply, a man of integrity, honest, ethical, and as moral as any individual she had ever worked for. Mr. Culpepper had been a mentor to Sandra and she had never forgotten how he helped to straighten a winding path on her journey to the principalship.

Dr. Rios recalled a lesson in words from her now deceased mentor: "Sandra, determine what tasks are to be done, who needs to do them, how the tasks are to be structured, who reports to whom, when and where decisions are to be made, and how *organized* you're willing to become? Remember, Sandra, successful principals move from learning and applying those qualities of leaders to becoming leaders of quality. Sandra, are you *prepared* to be a leader of quality?"

The last of the students had now passed from the common area, down the hallways, and into their classrooms. Sandra stood there, alone, smiling at the thought of how her mentor's lesson—in just a few words—had led her to complete her long and arduous journey toward a successful principalship.

Application Questions

1. A principal once shared with the authors of this text: "Be a yardstick of quality. Some people aren't accustomed to a leader who is prepared to expect excellence." How does this sentiment link to the skills of being daily organized and prepared when related to Principal Sandra Rios? What about Dr. Rios creates an impression that she is organized and prepared?
2. Ruminate on the old, anonymous adage: "The secret to success is being prepared to be organized." Using that quote as a point of reference, what can be inferred regarding Principal Sandra Rios relative to her earned reputation of being prepared and organized?
3. Reflect on the fifteen Likert scale listings on pages 29–30 of this chapter. Which one best relates to Principal Sandra Rios? Provide an explanation for your response.

4. Consider the areas of relevant leadership preparedness as detailed in the "7 Bs of Preparedness" section of the chapter. Explain which of the 7 Bs correlate to the actions and/or behaviors of Principal Sandra Rios?
5. Principals are known for what they repeatedly do. Thus, some would say that the skill of being daily organized is not an act but a habit. What might Principal Rios be doing on a daily basis that reveals she possesses the habit of being organized? Explain your answer.
6. Debate, in writing, the pros and cons of the following: No school leader, including Sandra Rios, can succeed in any great degree without being prepared.

Chapter 3

Daily Step #3
Lead, Delegate, but Never Dump!

"Leadership is not a position or title. It is action and example!"
—Unattributed

"The function of leadership is to produce more leaders, not more followers!" —Ralph Nader (in *Ralph Nader: A Man with a Mission*, 2002, by Nancy Bowen)

WHAT KIND OF LEADER DO YOU WANT TO BE?

The type of leadership incorporated impacts how a principal will view the school leader role and how a principal then interacts with colleagues. Principals have long been trained in the exploration of numerous leadership styles. Each principal leadership style has certain strengths and weaknesses (Johnson, 2016; Mitgang, 2008). Thousands of principal help books, along with more than 3.5 billion leadership and 4.8 million principal leadership style websites (Lynch, 2016) exist to aid in the focus of which *one* style serves as the best to expand a principal's mission, vision, and overall capabilities. In Table 3.1 is a brief description of nine principal leadership styles that current research studies detail (Cowan, 2018; Indeed Career Guide, 2019).

Interestingly, successful principals frequently transcend each of the nine noted leadership styles. Principals must incorporate different styles of school leadership at different times, all depending on the situation. Therefore, for a principal to be successful, every day, the school leader must regularly incorporate a common norm or style of leadership: Situational!

Table 3.1 Leadership Styles

Leadership Style	Description
Visionary	• Inspires, drives progress, ushers in periods of change • Earns trust for new ideas
Service	• Has a people-first perspective • Supports staff's personal and professional goals
Authoritarian/Autocratic	• Focuses entirely on results and efficiency • Usually the lone decision-maker • Expects staff to do exactly what is told/asked • Can impede innovation
Laissez-Faire	• Opposite of autocratic • Delegates tasks but fails to provide supervision • Faculty often have time to work on multiple projects with limited oversight
Democratic	• Collects and considers feedback from group • Fosters high levels of engagement
Transformational	• Focuses on communication, goal-setting, and employee motivation • Committed to organizational objectives • Examines the big picture with a visionary approach
Transactional	• Focuses on performance • Sets predetermined incentives and rewards for success, and disciplinary actions for failure • Focuses on mentorship, instruction, and training
Instructional	• Focuses efforts on improving teaching and learning
Situational	• Focuses on the significance of the situation and how a leader reacts and responds • The situation, not traits or abilities, plays the most important role in determining who emerges as a leader • Researchers advocate that leaders are made, not born—leadership forged on the basis of how one handles a situation

THE SITUATIONAL PRINCIPAL

School success hinges upon the rules and regulations that are in place to ensure all is running smoothly. Schools consist of a hierarchy of administrators, specialists, teachers, and support staff. Schools are also made up of students, as well as faculty and staff, of differing ages and numerous maturity levels. These multiple groups arrive at school with their own problems. Successful principals understand that any combination of people, attitudes, and/or emotions will readily lend itself to numerous issues, differing circumstances, or unique situations.

Successful principals understand and embrace many leadership styles during the course of a school day, all depending on the situation. This allows a principal to adapt to a leadership style that best suits the issue, circumstance, or situation. For example, successful principals frequently move from an autocratic leadership style, thus making decisions that impact the whole school, to a democratic style which encourages faculty and staff to collaboratively participate and engage in various initiatives and problem-solving processes.

Based on the situation, successful principals utilize a service style to connect with community partners while at the same time incorporating a visionary style to engage business, community, and district leaders relative to upcoming changes. Successful principals recognize that different situations, within the school and across the community, call for different styles of leadership.

Successful principals consistently revisit the different types of leadership styles and reflect upon past events and how incorporating a different style will encourage, if not completely enhance, results. A familiar assumption: Leaders are autocratic by nature. However, in a school environment, such an approach will readily wear thin with faculty, staff, parents, and students. A more productive approach occurs when a school leader carefully appraises the situation and calls upon an array of styles to alleviate difficult circumstances and associated issues and problems.

SHARED LEADERSHIP

An important aspect of successful principal leadership is daily recognizing the abilities of faculty and staff. A strong leader understands how to utilize the capabilities of colleagues to actively contribute to instructionally oriented discussions to aid assistant principals and team members in gaining better perspectives by encouraging active participation relative to simple or complex problems. Daily, the successful principal reviews upcoming events to determine if said activities are to be led by competent and capable faculty and staff. Successful principals share leadership responsibilities. This exercise helps a principal to evaluate where gaps in instruction or scheduling, for example, may occur.

Successful principals plan ahead. Principals must ask: "How can success be ensured and the longevity of committee work and instructional programs and other academic-related activities continue with a high-level of achievement?" Successful principals always consider faculty as potential leaders. Daily, principals must encourage those who show initiative to lead committees, pilot instructional initiatives, and guide professional development by offering continued direction, encouragement, and support. Listening to those engaged in shared leadership roles and responsibilities is one key to the making of a successful leading, teaching, and learning organization, and certainly, a successful school principal.

Successful principals encourage faculty and staff to create new instructionally-focused initiatives. Principals must bring new faculty along, albeit slowly, in this process. Successful principals always outline the first critical steps of any new initiative. These steps include: (a) an overview of the initiative; (b) the number of required faculty, staff, parents, corporate volunteers, and/or students to effectively and efficiently implement the initiative; (c) what materials will be required; (d) the identification of associated budgetary costs; and (e) who will be positively and, yes, negatively impacted. Successful principals continually add to this list as a means of ensuring more inclusivity, productivity, and organizational improvement.

Faculty need time to feel comfortable, gain confidence, and recognize how they are valued. The best principals make this happen. Successful principals, who carefully and actively listen to faculty and staff, will learn teacher interests, strengths, and weaknesses, and what particular leadership style(s) to incorporate when interacting with teachers, students, and even parents. Such an approach to school leadership will aid a principal in better utilizing faculty for shared leadership experiences and will ensure that faculty have essential skills to lend support and expertise to others—including the principal. Successful principals also recognize and understand prior experiences of faculty to best ensure that the right people are in the right position to do the right task at the right time. Such exemplifies outstanding shared leadership.

SUPPORTING NOVICE FACULTY

New and/or novice faculty bring a high level of energy to a school and moreover, have high personal expectations of teaching, leading, and learning roles. Novice teachers who have recently graduated from teaching programs arrive at a new school with a few ingrained perspectives: (1) experiences as an elementary, middle, and high school student which have impacted instructional thinking and teaching habits; (2) experiences from lessons during time in a university teacher preparation program which bring forth new ideals, research-based thinking and application, and a zeal to showcase new and different methods and strategies of instruction; (3) experiences with common media narratives concentrating on what schools, principals, and teaching life is all about; and (4) experiences as a student intern or teacher.

Current research reveals that most principals rarely interact with student teachers. While principals report that they do relate and connect with their student teachers, an otherwise unflattering picture emerges: principals, as reported in the research literature, spend minimal time with student teachers (Mungal, 2020a).

Regrettably, far too many principals delegate student teaching interactions and responsibilities to assistant principals, curriculum coordinators, academic coaches, and of course, teacher mentors. Successful principals take time to connect with student teachers to observe and provide crucial feedback as to how the student teachers are performing and adapting within the teaching and learning environment. This is an essential principal role and can actually serve to aid a principal who may be less familiar with current changes in teacher education programs. Such a good practice assists even the very best principals in maintaining an interest in research-based, best-practice, and student-centered educational initiatives.

It has long been acknowledged: "Knowledge is power!" Principal knowledge of current educationally-related and instructionally-oriented research is an absolute for a successful principalship, as well as a long-lasting career. Yukl and Gardner (2019) and Hughes, Ginnett, and Curphy (2019) have long espoused that with success comes power—a referent power, not an abusive power; an expert power, not a coercive power; a legitimate power, not a psychological tactic power; a position power, not a controlling-reward power. Using the best of these "powers," a principal will further enable the new energies of novice teachers. A principal and leadership team will utilize these new skills and novice teacher energies to best direct all faculty toward instructional excellence. Daily, successful principals work to match novice teachers with exceptional teacher mentors. The concept and application of mentoring will be examined later in this chapter.

Successful principals never forget that not only novice teachers, but also experienced teachers—who are new to a campus—will need time to acclimate to the school culture and leading, teaching, and learning environment. Whether admitted or not, here's an absolute: every school is different, every principal is different, and every team is different. It is often noted that "Students are students!" Yes and no. In actuality, every student is different!

Therefore, successful principals provide different types of support to aid the novice teacher or staff member in better understanding and thriving in the school setting. Remember, successful principals invest daily in new faculty because the dividends pay off immeasurably. Moreover, principal investment helps prepare novice teachers for bigger roles, greater responsibilities, and ultimately, distinguished careers.

INVESTING IN NEW AND EXPERIENCED FACULTY

Successful principals, as noted, invest in both new and experienced faculty. This investment permits team members to be empowered; it encourages new and better ideas; and investment leads to more and greater suggestions, recommendations, and solutions. Investing in and including novice faculty in decision-making and problem-solving builds community and continuity. Active investment and involvement equate to essential contributions!

Team contributions ensure that novice faculty are learning new skills—skills that ensure continuity. Continuity is a means by which skills gained are skills incorporated to further ensure both novice and experienced teachers implement a permanence in changes for further organizational improvement and overall student academic success. Change is difficult. A serious challenge for any principal is bringing long-needed and long-awaited change. Successful principals recognize early in their careers that the best changes come in incremental amounts because, as is well known: the only change humans like is that which jingles in their pocket!

One of the authors of this text describes, in the scenario below, one of his experiences as a high school teacher.

IN WITH THE NEW, OUT WITH THE OLD: A PRINCIPAL CONUNDRUM?

As the teacher population of Feldon Adams School was aging, experienced faculty, who had long organized and sponsored clubs, student-centered events and activities, and coached sport teams—many for 20 or more years—expressed feelings, privately and sometimes publicly, of stress and utter exhaustion. These team members had come to a singular conclusion: this commitment of time, energy, and interactions was taking a toll!

This group of exceptional faculty members needed a time to rest and recharge, or as one individual stated: "Get the hell out of dodge!" Many needed more than a road trip, a vacation, or a sabbatical. All needed a respite—at the very least, additional time with families. One individual, Copell Siegfried, said: "I've committed so much to our students that I've completely neglected my wife and kids—two kids who are now grown adults. They call me 'the absent father.'" A sad commentary but one that is much closer to the truth than personages outside of education realize.

Still others sought options to ease away from their long-term school/student commitments. "I've been at this too many years," another stated. But how could one ease away? Just quit? Some actually contemplated retirement, others resigned, as was the case with veteran teacher, Thaddeus Cuthbert. Cuthbert stated: "I've been chief sponsor of the chess club for seven years now. It's time to move on." Most of these long-tenured team members felt awkward approaching their principal. A few did, most did not. Question: What's a principal to do?

Successful principals regularly consider the toil of team member commitments, especially those that are long-term. Principals must realize that the very best educators continually work with students in academic, social, and athletic settings for the love of students, the love of seeing students achieve and succeed—all for the love of the game. For many, such passions have been instilled since their own days in school. Again, what's a principal to do when a change in faculty leadership and commitment is required?

Daily, successful principals anticipate change. They prepare. They establish lines of communications with faculty—these outstanding club and team organizers. Successful principals do so as a means of tracking potential changes. Positively, some changes occur through attrition. A new faculty member steps in and takes up a student-centered commitment. Regrettably, some changes that occur with attrition result in failure because a faculty member will not commit to the role and thus, organized events struggle to survive. Students are left behind with no recourse other than to disband the club or activity. Students move on to other activities—often outside of the school. Many of these outside activities are far from being in the best interests of students. Again, what's a principal to do?

Successful principals target daily new faculty and staff members to assist with the transitioning of staff to ensure that student-focused clubs, organizations, and activities continue. Early insertion of new or novice faculty into programs better ensures the learning of skills, and the gaining of knowledge to help sustain progress, programs, and student interest. By creating and maintaining open dialogue, successful principals are able to utilize faculty who show affinity and interest in supporting senior staff and thus, eventually step in, take charge, and coordinate the programs. Again, this ensures continuity and most important, supports the needs of students.

DELEGATING: A MENTORING ACT, NOT A DUMPING ACT

Successful principals will daily delegate to others key aspects of leading. This is an act of mentoring. Successful principals understand that organizational, if not leader achievement, is often built upon delegating duties. Principals work and lead in a hierarchal system of faculty, staff, administrators, support personnel, and volunteers. This system is purposefully designed to inform principals of the differing positions and duties held by personnel. Successful principals recognize that their daily communications and connections with other school-site members, through the delegation process, is a key to exceptional leadership and mentoring.

Having the right people in the right positions makes delegating duties that much easier. Delegating duties means that the successful principals who dedicate their time to leading a school know that the right people are in positions to better provide essential feedback, support, decision-making, and problem solving.

Successful principals know when to delegate duties and responsibilities to others, or when to support individuals as needed, or when to intervene and mentor personnel. Successful principals also delegate certain duties to members of the principals' leadership team. Remember, however, there is a fine line between delegating and dumping. No one appreciates being dumped on—ever! Two final notes: (1) Delegation is an integral part of mentoring. (2) Delegation is NEVER intended to be a ceremonial dumping of principal duties and responsibilities!

CONNECTING TO STUDENTS

Successful principals interact daily with students at all levels of schooling. Principals must connect with faculty and staff to learn more about students and vice versa!

Mentoring and supporting students is a vital component of successful leading, teaching, and learning. While *all* students need to be uplifted, effective mentoring aids in better ensuring student academic, social, and behavioral success. Successful principals target students who have been identified as high achievers to ensure that they are challenged. However, it is vital to also identify students who are at-risk, often falling through the cracks. These students must be encouraged through student mentorship programs to be better engaged, successful in learning, and ultimately, contribute positively to society.

Successful principals encourage students to participate in school events. The very best principals encourage students to actively participate in planning school events and activities. Such involvement, especially in the early grades, will have a long-term impact on student and organizational success.

The Center for Teaching and Learning (2019) supports student engagement by increasing their attention, focus, and motivation which leads to greater critical thinking skills. The Center also recommends service-learning which promotes student learning through a broad range of experiences (Center for Teaching and Learning, 2019).

Service-learning also impacts academic achievement, attendance, attitudes toward self, school and learning, as well as behavior, civil engagement, and social skills (Hopper, Sowers, Brinkley, Smith, & Saarnio, 2019). Service-learning is a powerful means of mentoring students across all educational levels.

FROM NEW PRINCIPALS TO SUCCESSFUL PRINCIPALS

New principals will not always have the confidence to trust that district policies, campus regulations, and principal-directed instructions are being carried out. New principals can easily gain reputations for micromanaging (DuFour & Mattos, 2013; Rigsbee, 2009). Successful principals, on the other hand, trust their leadership team and their staff. Some new principals will feel the need to micromanage. New principals, to be successful, must be aware of their micromanaging behaviors and make every effort to be clear about inquiring tendencies and further understanding how and why procedures are implemented.

Successful principals *learn* to be successful. The journey to success may not always be a smooth one, but self-reflection and communication go a long way in effecting success. New principals often fear being perceived as weak and indecisive. New principals must know that making quick decisions, before learning all the facts, can be dangerous, sometimes career ending. For a new principal to become a successful principal, the proper gathering of information is critical. This process includes, but is not limited to, speaking openly and honestly with all members of the learning community and consulting with experts at the school-site and/or district level.

New principals must form informal and formal networks to gain knowledge and establish community (Reyna, 2017). Formal district induction events allow new principals to engage colleagues. School districts also pair senior principals with novices to serve as mentors. However, these formal pairings can be a hit or miss proposition

Reyna (2017) points to the informal networks that form between novice and experienced principals which can serve as powerful support systems. Most novice principals experience numerous new, different, and difficult issues that informal mentoring, with experienced principals, can often resolve. Consulting with colleagues at other schools and maintaining the formal and informal networks will add, over time, to new principal resolve and experience and thus, better ensure an open road to a successful principalship. A recommended source is *With Great Power Comes Great Responsibility: Navigating Year One of the Principalship*, by Dr. Angela Reyna (ProQuest, 2017).

ENCOURAGEMENT, INSPIRATION, AND MOTIVATION

No principal has ever gone through a day incident free. Arguments, frustrations, and anger spill out when dealing with the diverse maturity levels and personalities of individuals who make up the learning community. School personnel are also susceptible to bad and stressful days. Successful principals must be aware and connected to their school's personnel and understand how climate and culture impact a school principal and personnel as vital factors affecting perceptions, ideas, values, beliefs, and behaviors (Bharthvajan, 2019; Sorenson & Goldsmith, 2009). Successful principals are always problem-solvers and decision-makers.

Successful principals must also encourage, inspire, and motivate. School personnel are not always aware of the myriad of administrative problem-solving and decision-making that principals make every day. Successful principals buffer campus personnel from the pressures of outside interfering sources. Successful principals understand that visibility is a great motivator. Successful principals use visibility as a means of meeting, and greeting, and constantly interacting with students, teachers, parents, and community members.

Additionally, visibility allows a principal to see and hear first-hand curricular issues, student problems, physical plant circumstances, and personnel situations that might otherwise go unnoticed by the school leader. Unnoticed, unchecked, or unseen—but call it what it is, because principals who ignore "visibility" as a leadership tool will be unable to provide sound guidance and leader direction, which will further erode confidence in the principal and, thus, ensure what began as a minor, if not trivial or possibly petty issue, will deteriorate into a significantly more acute problem!

By being visible, successful principals are able to move about offering support and recognition to students, personnel, and parents. Successful principals also utilize the time to meet with leadership groups within the school to obtain updates, offer support, problem solve, and even make personnel changes—bringing in new personnel to help with instructional gaps, curriculum dilemmas, and other ever-mounting quandaries.

A daily key to becoming a successful leader is ensuring that all parties collaboratively interact to share views, ideas, and concerns. Successful principals utilize a clear and positive language to elicit a collaborative team spirit and unity. Collaborative principals resoundingly signal a clear and crucial message: "I'm here to work with you!"

However, collaborative leadership never negates high expectations or the fact that a principal must ask the hard questions about teaching, leading, and learning. Remember, tough decisions, even in a collaborative environment, will always be required. Unrelenting problems will always be at hand. Yet, successful principals always persevere as lead collaborators and facilitators who are daily prepared to encourage, inspire, and motivate!

TRUST BUT VERIFY

President Ronald Reagan borrowed the Russian proverb "Doveryai, no proveryai" (*Trust but verify*) to describe the relationship to the two superpowers that led to *glasnost* (openness and transparency). In this case, we use the phrase "trust but verify" as a navigational tool to support school personnel and also to check on whether the goals of the school and the classroom are being met. Successful principals set the parameters for success by consistently ensuring that personnel are being proactively engaged in all aspects of the curricular and instructional program. Successful principals maintain success by validating that everyone is working up to and even beyond their potential.

Success has been described as not waiting for an opportunity. It's all about creating it! Remember, a leader's greatest weakness lies not in failure but in simply giving up. Success comes when an individual is always willing to try just one more time. Are you ready to try? Are you willing to lead?

FINAL THOUGHTS

Successful principals frequently adopt different leadership styles, all depending on the situation. The best principals regularly revisit different types of leadership styles, visionary, service, authoritarian or autocratic, laissez-faire, democratic, transformational, transactional, instructional, and situational.

Successful principals capitalize at the school-site level by investing in students and school personnel. Strong school leaders recognize early in their careers that shared leadership must be a daily exercise in evaluating any aspect of the instructional program. These principals encourage faculty and staff to take the lead in creating new instructionally focused initiatives, always outlining purposeful steps which allow for effective and efficient program implementation.

Successful principals support novice faculty, recognizing that new personnel bring a high level of energy and personal expectations to the teaching, leading, and learning roles. The very best school leaders interact regularly with not only new faculty but also with student teachers who are on campus, learning the ropes. Daily, successful principals work to match novice teachers and, yes, student teachers, with exceptional teacher mentors. Exceptional principals invest daily in new faculty as the dividends are all too frequently positively immeasurable.

Successful principals anticipate change. They are prepared to lead via open lines of communication, daily and purposefully targeting faculty and staff who will assist with change transitioning to best ensure that instructional, operational, and organizational activities remain constant and in place, all to benefit students. These school leaders recognize community outreach must accompany any proposed change. Better community relationships allow for mutual assistance and learning to aid in solving political, social, behavioral, and economical issues and problems.

Successful principals will mentor—on a daily basis—faculty, staff, and students. Novice teachers, as well as incoming new, but experienced, teachers must be engaged in strong mentorship programs. Successful principals are always seeking opportunities to build a program of effective mentoring, to include but not limited to delegating responsibilities to others. Such is an act of effective mentoring.

Successful principals connect daily with students. All students need to be uplifted, and mentoring helps students achieve academically, socially, and behaviorally. The principal-student connection serves as a positive encouragement to students, better ensuring they actively participate in school events and activities. Such has a long-term impact as connectivity engages students in the learning process, increases their attention and focus, motivates achievement, and leads to high-level critical thinking skills.

DISCUSSION QUESTIONS

1. Identify examples of principal leadership styles observed at the school-site level. How did the identified styles impact the school leader role?
2. Research reveals that shared leadership enhances the likelihood of change acceptance. Of the five steps (see page 40) critical to successful instructional change or initiative acceptance, which two do you believe are most impactful to better ensuring personnel reception?
3. Outline why supporting novice faculty is essential to their personal success as well as the success of the instructional program and ultimately, student achievement?
4. How can a principal best invest in not only novice faculty, but also in experienced faculty as well? Explain.
5. Identify techniques or strategies for successful principal-student interaction/connectivity. Explain how said approaches enhance student motivation and learning.
6. Explain the difference between the delegating of and the dumping of principal/leadership-oriented tasks on others. How can a principal better ensure delegation is not perceived as dumping?
7. Consider the following: "visibility"—"trust but verify"—"inspect what you expect." Explain the connectivity of each relative to the development of a strong, student-centered instructional program, as well as a successful principalship.

CASE STUDY APPLICATION—
"AND I WANTED TO BE A SCHOOL PRINCIPAL!"

Molly Raj is the new principal at Scarborough High School. The population of the school is more than 2,250 students, with a faculty and staff of 117. The new principal leads a strong administrative team as well as a competent instructional faculty.

One of the campus teachers, O'Reilly Day, volunteers to lead a campus-related project. As time progresses, he is unable to move the project forward. Mr. Day prefers to wait until Principal Raj provides him with specific direction. He also seeks excessive principal recognition and approval. He requires continued encouragement from his new principal.

Another campus teacher, Rudy Mohan, volunteers to work on a similar, yet different, campus-related project. Rudy is most capable of not only initiating the work but also completing the essential tasks prior to the deadline imposed by Principal Raj. However, Mr. Mohan is a Type-A personality who pushes, if not offends, different campus personnel with his highly ambitious, competitive, controlling, determined, and demanding approach to task management and completion. Notably, he really irritates the normally unperturbed assistant principal, Vanessa Baya, a classic Type-B personality!

Vanessa Baya is highly competent and capable in her role. She is flexible and typically laid-back, but she can become quite expressive, if not emotional—especially when working with Rudy Mohan. Nevertheless, Vanessa is a nice complement to Principal Raj and the other assistant principals. Most recently, Vanessa and Rudy have "locked horns" over the direction of the project Rudy leads. Less than pleasant words were exchanged. Neither is willing to apologize, and both insist that Principal Raj resolve the situation.

Returning to O'Reilly Day: Principal Raj believes that O'Reilly is more than capable of handling and completing the required instructionally-oriented task. However, he is continually unwilling to begin a project without his new principal convincing him that it is alright to proceed. Mr. Day also expects Principal Raj to dictate explicit steps required for project development and completion.

Rudy Mohan requires no such assistance. No prodding, and certainly no convincing he's doing a good job. Rudy states to Assistant Principal Vanessa Baya: "I've got more experience than you, and I don't need you interfering with this project! Go and take care of O'Reilly. He always needs to be persuaded that he's doing right! I don't need convincing—I know I'm doing right! Be gone with you! Got it, kiddo?" Rudy Mohan then heads towards Principal Raj's office. Assistant Principal Baya seethes! Close to tears, she hollers down the hallway at Rudy: "You just go and tattle to Ms. Raj. See if I care. We'll see who'll head this project and I'll promise you this—it won't be you!"

Then, the assistant principal turns around and looks down the hallway. The hallway is teeming with students who are staring and absolutely silent, if not shocked. Then, one of the students laughs and hollers out: "Way to go, Miss. You tell him!" Vanessa Baya, now red-faced with anger and embarrassment, instructs the students to move along to their classes. Usually relaxed and less than stressed, the assistant principal recognizes this is a situation that has gone from bad to worse and she's as much to blame as Rudy Mohan. She thinks to herself: "I really don't have the time to take on Rudy's project. Plus, why do I let my emotions get the best of me? Ms. Raj doesn't need this added worry!"

Principal Raj, sitting at her desk, contemplates the issue with O'Reilly Day. She realizes he is a follower who lacks self-confidence, independent commitment, personal motivation, and self-respect. Rudy Mohan quietly steps into the administrative office of Principal Raj as she mumbles out loud: "His psychological maturity for completing job-related tasks is sorely lacking!" Rudy Mohan looks at his principal in amazement: "Are you talking about me? Look, Molly, my psychological maturity is off the chart and I don't need a medical opinion from you! Consider talking to your assistant principal. If anyone is psychologically immature, it's Vanessa!" Molly Raj looks up, startled, and simply shakes her head in annoyance and says: "Rudy, give me a break! I'm not talking about you or Vanessa. Don't you have a project to attend to?"

Principal Molly Raj has three very different issues and personalities with which to contend. Each circumstance or situation demands the principal's time and attention. At times, Molly is on the verge of exploding when interacting with each of the three team members. However, she's a professional and holds her tongue, realizing that her leadership style with each individual all depends upon the situation. With each of the employees mentioned, Principal Raj must not only focus on the three campus followers, collectively and independently, but also on each situation. The campus leader thinks to herself: "And I wanted to be a school principal!"

Application Questions

1. Initiate, in writing, a brief developmental process as related to "participating in" and "completing" task-oriented work. Associate the process with the aiding of each of the individuals and situations involved. Consider O'Reilly Day, teacher; Rudy Mohan, teacher; and Vanessa Baya, assistant principal. Now, think as a successful principal would: How can these individuals be assisted to help make each one a better leader and team player? Be specific in your analyses.
2. Should Principal Molly Raj initiate a development plan or process for herself and/or ask her supervisor or a principal mentor to aid her in doing so? Why or why not? Explain.
3. Each of the three situations in the scenario relate to at least one of the following behaviors. Determine which individual (O'Reilly Day, Rudy

Mohan, Vanessa Baya, or Molly Raj) best correlates with which of the identified professional behavior deficiencies. Explain how and why.
_____ participating in and completing tasks
_____ task instructions—telling and directing
_____ strong encouragement
_____ support and endorsement
_____ task reductions
_____ accomplishing delegated tasks
_____ principal time and commitment
_____ status control and patience
_____ stress-induced, emotional outbursts
_____ low relationship oriented, high task motivated
_____ perceptive listening, encouraging, facilitating, and clarifying skills
_____ redirection/refocus of knowledge relevance, experience, and skills
_____ enhanced or improved personal and professional interactions

4. Return to the beginning of the chapter and reflect upon each of the leadership styles and descriptors as noted in Table 3.1. Then, consider the above-noted scenario and answer the following questions:
   - Which leadership style(s) is most depicted by Principal Molly Raj?
   - Which leadership style(s) should Principal Molly Raj incorporate when working with O'Reilly Day, teacher? Why?
   - Which leadership style(s) should Principal Molly Raj utilize when interacting with Rudy Mohan, teacher? Why?
   - Which leadership style(s) should Principal Molly Raj apply when interacting with her assistant principal, Vanessa Baya? Why?
5. Is the depicted scenario realistic? Why or why not? Be detailed in your answer.
6. Relate Principal Molly Raj to the chapter segment about shared leadership along with supporting novice faculty and staff. Is this new principal seizing upon successful leadership tendencies described in this chapter as well as those in previous chapters? Explain.
7. How can Principal Raj best encourage, inspire, or motivate these three different personalities: O'Reilly Day, Vanessa Baya, and Rudy Mohan? Explain.

Concluding Point

Years ago, one of the authors of this text was given pointed advice by a superintendent of schools: "Successful leadership all depends on the situation and how you handle it." Your thoughts?

Chapter 4

Daily Step #4

Anticipate, Adjust, and Learn

"No plan of operations reaches, with any certainty, beyond the first encounter with the enemy's main force." —Helmuth van Moltke, Prussian Military Commander, in Kriegsgechichtiche Einzelschriften (1880), Oxford Reference, Susan Ratcliffe, editor

ANTICIPATING THE WORK DAY AND WORK WEEK

Principals' work days never seem to end. Some events actually make a principal feel like the school leader is experiencing déjà-vu once again (Berra, 2010). Others simply run into each other making it harder to distinguish one problem from another, unless principals are willing to anticipate, adjust, and learn. Successful principals are constantly aware of the commitments and sacrifices it takes to operate a school. Successful principals and teams plan out events for the whole school year. With an overall plan in place, successful principals will ensure a solid organizational and operational foundation.

However, educators know—as has been explored previously in chapter 2—no matter how much time is spent preparing for school events and adhering to the schedules, the unexpected happens. Successful principals recognize that the unexpected must be expected! Therefore, long-term and short-term planning is essential for the smooth operation of a school.

Successful principals establish personal time before the arrival of students and personnel to become centered—focused, balanced, and adjusted—all in anticipation of what's to come! Some principals begin their day with exercise—walking, jogging, or going to the gym. Others choose to arrive at school and read their favorite electronic news source or inspirational or spiritual daily devotion. Daily, successful principals seek methods and practices to better anticipate and prepare for the rapidly approaching school day. What practice do you use to center yourself?

Monday brings about a new, positive energy to start the week! Successful principals start the school week anticipating upcoming events. These principals begin each week setting aside time in the morning to review the weekly and daily schedule. Successful principals establish a Monday morning meeting to ensure that leadership is prepared for upcoming events. This time is used to go over all planned weekly activities, and to confirm that everything is properly staffed. The principal will also use this first weekly meeting to bring up any new agenda items and inquire on the progress of ongoing plans, practices, initiatives, instructional or behavioral concerns, and/or personnel issues. Successful principals always anticipate, consider, adjust, and learn. They seriously contemplate the potential for any sudden issue or problem and adapt accordingly to last minute changes. Finally, they conclude the work week with a Friday meeting as a weekly wrap-up session.

Successful principals set aside time within the Monday weekly meeting to reflect upon the events of the previous week. Successful principals encourage other campus administrators, as well as academic coaches, to share lessons from past events to help inform the team relative to current and future events. Solutions to curricular, instructional, and other issues often occur if proper reflection is not only a weekly but a daily process.

Successful principals discuss past events to see what went right and wrong to help ensure future success. Just because an event is successful does not mean that lessons cannot be learned. Daily, successful principals and teams are open to discussing changes to past procedures. With hindsight, successful principals and teams can anticipate and predict future events and issues.

CHECKING THE PULSE

Each day, successful principals are instrumental in setting the mood of the school. Reflect back to chapter 3 and the descriptions of ensuring a daily visible presence. Simply walking across campus and meeting and greeting students, teachers, and parents can be a very revealing process. This casual act can lower barriers, promote conversations, and allow a principal to anticipate problems, adjust thinking and/or misperceptions, solve dilemmas, and learn—learn what's happening when, where, and why.

Seeing a principal out and about permits personnel to be more comfortable by speaking up in what is recognized as a casual, conversational interaction with the school leader. Successful principals recognize that these casual conversations, rather than those that are more formal in an office setting, permit the school leader, using a keen listening ear, to pick up on information—positive and negative—and therefore gauge the level of potential school-related problems.

Successful principals also encourage the leadership team to be visible on and across campus. The principal knows that some personnel will be more comfortable speaking to different leadership administrators. The end result is that leadership visibility encourages communication. With communication comes collaboration. With collaboration comes open and positive interaction. Engaging, communicating, collaborating, and interacting with personnel sends a strong and vital message: The principal is available, approachable, and cares.

MINDFULNESS

The term "mindfulness" is evocative of being present in the moment. Mindfulness reminds school leaders to observe personal and the professional thoughts and feelings of self and others. Mindfulness is associated with the lowering of stress and has been associated with reducing depression and anxiety (*Psychology Today*, 2019). While there is a holistic approach to mindfulness, Weick and Sutcliffe (2001) have connected mindfulness to a more business and management perspective. Both perspectives can aid a principal in becoming more successful.

Key characteristics of mindfulness have been identified by Weick and Sutcliffe as possessing: (a) a concern for potential failure, (b) a keenness to never simplify early or frequent interpretations, (c) a sensitivity to effective operations, (d) a commitment to resilience, and (e) a deference to expertise (see Table 4.1).

Weick and Sutcliffe also examined resilience within highly reliable organizations (HROs) such as hospital emergency rooms, nuclear power plants, and aircraft carriers. Such organizations operate under extreme pressure and stress and do so mindfully. School leaders can learn to anticipate, manage, and adjust to the unexpected events that occur every day. Weick and Sutcliffe's work is relevant because schools have long transitioned from a managerial sphere of leadership to one where instructional accountability is the dominant force in principal leadership and schooling.

Finally, Weick and Sutcliffe recommend that organizations heed early and troubling signals and respond proactively to first signs. Being mindful means anticipating and recognizing early symptoms, albeit initially weak, yet troubling. Initial and worrisome signals are just that—disconcerting precursors of what's to come.

School personnel often "test" the patience of a principal and leadership team by toiling to effectively sabotage programs and initiatives. Daily, successful principals proactively respond to such actions by looking for early signals. Successful principals ensure a dedicated and powerful response. Bottom line: mindfulness will inform principals of potential problems before they begin. Remember—anticipate, adjust, and learn!

Table 4.1 Mindfulness: Characteristics and Explanations

Characteristic	Explanation
Preoccupation with Failure	• Treat every lapse as a symptom that something is wrong with the system. • HROs encourage reporting of errors to superiors.
Reluctance to Simplify Interpretations	• HROs take deliberate steps to create more complete and nuanced pictures. They simplify less and see more. • They encourage people with diverse experiences, skepticism toward accepted wisdom, and negotiating tactics reconcile differences. • If there is no diversity, everyone sees the same warning signals and is blind to the same unexpected warnings.
Sensitivity to Operations	• HROs have an ongoing concern with the unexpected. They are attentive to the front line, where the real work gets done.
Commitment to Resilience	• No system is perfect. HROs complement their learning from failure, complicating their perceptions, and remaining sensitive to operations with a commitment to resilience. • HROs develop capabilities to detect, contain, and bounce back from inevitable errors. • The signature of an HRO is not that it is error-free, but the errors don't disable it. • Here resilience means keeping errors small and improvising workarounds that keep the system functioning.

Deference to Expertise	• HROs cultivate diversity because it helps them notice more in complex environments but also helps them to cope with the complexities they spot.
	• HROs push decision making down.
	• Decisions are made on the front line.
	   ○ Authority migrates to the people with the most expertise, regardless of rank.
	   ○ This isn't about deferring to people with experience, as experience is no guarantee of expertise.

Source: Weick & Sutcliffe, 2001.

Schools, like many organizations, have culturally accepted beliefs, norms, policies, regulations, procedures, and rules—all of which can be stretched, bent, melded, and even broken. Identified below are three categories with 15 recommendations that will assist principals in managing those unexpected events which threaten to "break" some aspect of schooling.

CULTURE, GOALS, AND HONESTY: PRINCIPAL GUIDES TO BETTER ANTICIPATING, ADJUSTING, AND LEARNING

Being ever-mindful, daily, successful principals examine three categories which enhance the overall effectiveness of a teaching, leading, and learning community.

School Culture—Principals must:

1. Preserve a balance of values that are communicated through actions, reactions, and decisions.
2. Restate school goals in the form of mistakes that must not occur.
3. Remember that mindfulness takes effort. Therefore, school personnel must pay attention to failures as well as successes.
4. Review and revise existing practices. This allows a principal to encapsulate new experiences and fight complacency and rigidity.

School Goals—Principals must:

1. Create an awareness of vulnerability. Successful principals sensitize employees to the possibility of unexpected errors that can escalate into major problems. People need to worry about vulnerability and feel accountable for reliability. This awareness serves to increase opportunities for better teaching, improved learning, and more effective leadership.
2. Create an error-friendly leading, teaching, and learning environment. Seek feedback, share information, and encourage the asking of help and learning from mistakes.
3. Encourage open and honest conversations. Just because an individual observes something that is inhibiting learning doesn't mean someone else observes it too.
4. Support interpersonal skills and establish strengthening conflict resolution skills.

Stay Honest. It is, by the way, the best policy! Principals must:

1. Cultivate humility and be wary of overconfidence. Arrogance is a camouflage for insecurity. Arrogance actually diminishes wise thinking. Arrogance will make a principal fall.
2. Principals must be humble and remain humble. Finally, there's a fine line between confidence and arrogance—it's called humility. Know the line, see the line. Remember, confidence smiles, arrogance smirks!
3. Be glad for bad days. When things go wrong, principals have the opportunity to uncover more details and thus, learn. Pessimism is more mindful than optimism.
4. Support skeptics. Skeptics make independent efforts to confirm issues, giving a school leader two sets of observations. Skepticism counteracts complacency and provides a nuanced description.
5. Be suspicious of good news. There is always bad news and if you get no bad news, someone is hiding something.

6. Seek out bad news. Subordinates are much more likely to report good news to superiors. Why? It's better to report good news than face the potential for change because of bad news.
7. Welcome uncertainty. Uncertainty means a principal is in touch with reality.
8. Establish high expectations. When an unanticipated event actually occurs, a successful principal will soon, if not immediately, spot shortfalls in understanding. Successful principals need to keep updating and revising expectations—never lowering.

Developing a strong and successful school culture, establishing *S*pecific, *M*easurable, *A*chievable, *R*ealistic, and *T*ime-bound (*SMART*) school goals, and always staying honest are characteristics of successful principals who incorporate into daily leadership these categories as processes to bring about the following effective principal leadership and instructional team norms. The best principals and teams establish:

- Clear organizational purpose and student-centered instructional priorities;
- Well-defined personnel roles and responsibilities;
- Equity of voice and active participation of all parties—faculty, staff, students, and parents;
- Planned goals and objectives which are regularly addressed (remember, "trust but verify");
- Informed decision-making and problem-solving based on regular data analysis;
- Constant reviews of campus action or improvement plans to determine if goals, objectives, ownership, and due dates are being identified and met; and
- Systematic and consistent tracking expectations as a means of monitoring both implementation and success (remember, "inspect what you expect!").

ADJUSTING FOR EVERYDAY EVENTS

School environments, in recent years, have become much faster paced. Emergencies and last-minute issues push against pre-arranged meetings, schedules, and timetables. So, today, what is essential for organizational success? Strong leadership, clear mission, and instructional teams which can take on shared leadership responsibilities. Many schools incorporate academic coaches. These individuals assist principals by providing instructional expertise. Academic or instructional coaches must be detail-oriented, yet big-picture (visionary) thinkers. They must possess a clear mindset when establishing student-centered, instructionally-focused teaching and learning environments. They must be resilient and compelling leaders! These individuals must also be exceptional analyzers of data, as well as supportive and loyal team players.

Academic coaches must work in tandem with the school principal in developing the school's action or improvement plan. These instructional leaders aid principals in curriculum development, alignment, and renewal processes. They also ensure that teachers are incorporating and following the campus action or improvement plan—always anticipating, monitoring, and adjusting teacher instructional methods and techniques, student academic progress, and program planning procedures.

Academic coaches assist and support campus principals by enhancing the development and leveraging of ongoing/on-campus professional development. These lead learners help teachers and staff plan and execute impactful professional development to better ensure faculty remain up-to-date regarding the latest in research-based, student-centered, and best-practice initiatives.

Academic coaches build teacher and instructional capacity (see chapter 7), always focusing on student learning and achievement. They develop strong teacher/student/coach relationships, always training each group to learn and succeed through enhanced data analysis. Academic coaches help principals by making necessary—and sometimes sudden—adjustments in teaching and learning techniques and strategies.

Academic coaches are often the "right-hand" people to a school principal. They establish effective two-way communication with faculty and staff and principal, involving all in the process of instructionally-oriented problem-solving and decision-making. Recall the adage revealed in earlier chapters: "All of us are smarter than any one of us!" A most important aspect of the communication process, as enhanced by academic coaches, is "reflective" learning. Here, the coaches encourage teachers and team members, by example, to daily reflect and then take essential, if not critical, action to improve teaching, learning, and even leading.

Adjusting is an ever-present aspect of campus leading, teaching, and learning. Successful principals depend on individuals who are in service as academic coaches. Some of the very best principals will reveal in a heartbeat who they depend on most, and from whom they learn frequently—academic coaches.

One principal we know recently stated: "I'm a strong instructional leader and facilitator. But, I'm so fortunate to have my academic coaches. They are highly evolved from an instructional standpoint. They regularly sit in or lead instructional leadership team meetings as well as professional learning community (PLC) team meetings, especially when adjustments must be made—adjustments usually caused or created by me!" (Sorenson & Mungal, 2019).

The same principal further stated: "Frequently, I'm called to the district offices for training with consultants or other experts, or I have to attend meetings with the superintendent or area superintendent. Being a school leader is all about adapting and adjusting to a role that is constantly changing, relentlessly headed in one direction, then radically about-faced in another direction. Losing our campus academic coaches would be catastrophic to me: like cutting off one of my arms—maybe both" (Sorenson & Mungal, 2019).

HANDLING CRISES

Violent attacks on schools across the United States have been on the rise. Embedded in our collective conscience are Columbine, Sandy Hook, and Marjory Stoneman Douglas. These attacks are meant to strike fear and terrorize the most vulnerable population—children. As a result, district and campus leaders have initiated greater efforts to ensure school security. Despite increased precautions, district administrators and school principals must be ever-vigilant to potential disruptions, disturbances, and attacks.

Administrators, too, can be victims of disruptive incidents, if not attacks, that are in reality now viewed as normalized—angry parents, community members, and certain unsettling local events. These types of incidents are usually addressed through dialogue. Unfortunately, interactive discussions are not always the remedy or outcome to settling a dispute. However, with a greater emphasis on school safety, principals must be absolute in their resolve that small disruptions do not escalate into schoolwide disturbances or attacks!

The very nature of school responses has changed. For many decades, schools prepared for potential emergencies via the fire-drill where students would file out of the building and move to "designated" areas on school grounds or to a neutral and nearby site. There was a time when fire-drills were planned with school personnel often anticipating the event.

We recall fire-drills as typically being haphazard in nature and frequently welcomed by students who heralded the drill as time away from the boredom of teaching and learning. Teachers often felt the entire procedure was a waste of valuable instructional time. Times have changed—see the inset below.

A NOT-SO-FUNNY LOOK AT AN OLD, NOW NEW SCHOOL RULE

No gu~~m~~ n

Sadly, if not tragically, times have changed

Over the past 30 years, district leaders, principals, and teams have adopted many school security measures. The Department of Homeland Security (DHS) has several links and downloadable PDFs that can support current school safety policies at www.dhs.gov/cisa/school-safety-and-security. The Department of Homeland Security recommends a Targeted Violence Prevention Plan. Part of this plan is a threat assessment process which requires principals to identify troubling students, calculate their risk for participating in violence or other detrimental activities, and identify intervention strategies to handle the potential for risk (Department of Homeland Security, 2019).

The Targeted Violence Prevention Plan presents seven steps that successful principals can utilize to strengthen their own policies. The plan is summarized in Table 4.2 and it is highly recommended that principals and teams access Enhancing School Safety Using a Threat Assessment Model: An Operational Guide for Preventing Targets School Violence available at www.dhs.gov/sites/default/files/publications/18_0711_USSS_NTAC-Enhancing-School-Safety-Guide.pdf.

Table 4.2   A Step-by-Step Violence Prevention Plan

Step	Definition
Step 1: Establish a Multidisciplinary Threat Assessment Team	Team of school personnel—faculty, staff, administrators, coaches and available resource officers—to direct, manage, and document the threat assessment process.
Step 2: Define Behaviors	Behaviors that are prohibited and should trigger immediate intervention (e.g., threats, violent acts, weapons) and other concerning behaviors.
Step 3: Establish and Provide Training on a Central Reporting System	Establish and provide training on a central reporting system such as school website, email address, phone, apps. Ensure anonymity for those reporting and be monitored and will follow-up reports.
Step 4: Determine Threshold for Law Enforcement Intervention	Establish when law enforcement is necessary, especially if there is a safety risk.
Step 5: Establish Threat Assessment Procedures	Establish procedures to maintain documentation, identify information sources, reviewing records, and conducting interviews.
Step 6: Develop Risk Management Options	Develop risk management options to enact once an assessment is complete. Create individualized management plans to mitigate identified risks. Notify law enforcement immediately if student is thinking about an attack, ensure the safety of potential targets, create a situation less prone to violence, redirect the student's motive, and reduce the effect of stressors.
Step 7: Create and Promote a Safe School Climate	Build a culture of safety, respect, trust, and emotional support. Encourage communication, intervene in conflicts and bullying, and empower students to share concerns.

While the DHS website provides a wide range of recommendations and solutions, successful principals understand the character of their schools, students, and communities. Identified below are two perspectives that principals must consider when engaging law enforcement agents.

1. *News reports* have exposed instances, in schools, where violence, bullying, assault, and police brutality have occurred. Principals must be aware of district policies to best ensure appropriate and crucial safety communications with not only district personnel, but also with law enforcement as well. Today, social media has become extremely powerful. Events and incidents are posted in real time, placing added pressures on administrators and police officers. This phenomenon is examined in greater detail in chapter 8.
2. *Law enforcement involvement.* Successful principals are aware of what has been an escalation of tensions when law enforcement officials become forcefully entangled in school-site disturbances or disruptions. Students of color are more likely than their White peers to be arrested. When overall enrollment is considered, "the disparities are even more severe" (Blad & Harwin, 2017).

Even though Black students make up only 15.5% of overall enrollment, they are arrested at a rate of 33.4%, while Hispanic students (24.7% enrollment) are arrested at a rate of 24.9% (Blad & Harwin, 2017). Civil rights activists postulate students of color often bear the burden of retaliatory zero-tolerance policies and state laws which often cause arrests for moderately minor misbehavior, such as vandalism or classroom disagreements (Blad & Harwin, 2017).

When police are in communities of color, they criminalize behavior that wouldn't normally be the case—notably in White enclaves, relates Alison Brown, the executive director of the Communities for Just Schools Fund and a former lawyer for the U.S. Department of Justice (Blad & Harwin, 2017). Civil rights and student groups argue that police don't belong in schools, while school leaders, community leaders, parents, and police groups state they are necessary for overall security (Blad & Harwin, 2017).

However, principals must be aware that there is now increased scrutiny of the role of police in schools with the release of several videos showing police abuse of students (Blad & Harwin, 2017). Successful principals are aware of the potential for such interactions and recognize and respond to the "continuing inequalities for students of color, including greater school suspensions rates, inadequate opportunities to be taught by experienced instructors, and thus, all too infrequent access to a higher level of teaching and learning" (Blad & Harwin, 2017).

Successful principals actively communicate with law enforcement officials to ensure that officers know and understand all aspects of the learning community. Connecting with local police and inviting them onto the school grounds will familiarize officers with students and personnel. Such builds trust, familiarity, and respect among all parties. Proactively extending invitations allows for less adversarial confrontations between students and law enforcement officials.

MINDFUL OF "TOP-DOWN" DICTATES AND DEMANDS: PRINCIPALS ON THE "FRONTLINE"

Principals are in unique positions of power. They garner a great deal of independence when making schoolwide decisions relative to students, personnel, and programs. However, principals are subject to district policies, superintendent decisions, and school board choices. Successful principals are mindful as to how to carefully, prudently, and effectively navigate through the policies and demands placed upon them. Many demands are top-down. As a result, principals are on the frontline and must be ever-mindful of the crucial need to implement policies, gather critical data, and respond in a timely and appropriate manner to those daily top-down demands.

Top-down dictates and demands often create high expectations for principals, and at times, stress. Successful principals understand how to not only comply with but also how to categorize dictates and demands into manageable tasks and courses of action. These principals are also prepared to translate "top-down" directives into viable, if not recognizable, portions for uncomplicated learning community consumption and acceptance.

UNDERSTANDING SIMILAR EVENTS MAY HAVE DIFFERENT OUTCOMES

Principals can, at times, run the risk of complacency, especially if a principal comes to view each day and week as a repetition of the other. However, a cautionary measure for all principals is to anticipate and acknowledge that similar events can very well have different outcomes. Successful principals are able to adjust during the course of a "normal" day or week when faced with an unexpected or different outcome. In fact, a successful principal is proactive, often anticipating, if not expecting, the potential for a setback. When this happens, contingencies must be in place. As a reminder, the very best principals anticipate, adjust, and learn!

Daily, a successful principal interacts with school personnel who act as the leader's additional set of "eyes and ears" to better ensure that a principal expects the unexpected and is prepared to handle any circumstance in a proper and timely manner. The successful principal can also rely on the leadership team to make immediate and effective decisions when problem-solving unexpected predicaments. The successful principal can also ensure that prospective issues are discussed in both informal and formal meetings prior to the conceivable becoming achievable. The successful principal must trust the leadership team to recognize faults in the system.

FINAL THOUGHTS

Daily, successful principals anticipate, adjust, and learn from situations and circumstances that occur at the school-site level. Principals must be centered and well-adjusted in their role as campus leaders. Serious contemplation for any potential or sudden issue or problem and then adapting accordingly makes for a successful principalship.

Successful principals establish the culture and climate of schools. They are mood-setters, seeking out personnel in casual, conversational interactions, always maintaining a keen listening ear in order to gauge the level of potential school-related problems. Visibility, communication, and collaboration send a strong and vital message to all stakeholders: The principal is available, approachable, and cares! Successful principals are mindful—possessing a concern for potential problems, a keenness of oversimplification, a sensitivity to proper operational effectiveness, a commitment to resilience, and a deference to on- and off-campus expertise.

Successful principals, on a daily basis, develop an open school culture, establish student-centered SMART goals and objectives, and remain honest—individuals of integrity (please refer to page 58). These leaders maintain a clear organizational purpose, develop well-defined personnel roles and responsibilities, permit an equity of voice and participation, make informed decisions, and solve problems based on regular data analysis. Successful principals "trust but verify" and always "inspect what they expect"!

Daily, successful principals adjust; they expect the unexpected, anticipating and preparing, and frequently incorporating the expertise of school-site academic coaches. These coaches enhance and lead, with strong principal involvement, professional development. They collaborate with all personnel as well as the school principal. Academic coaches serve the learning community by adjusting curriculum and instruction to meet the varied needs of all students.

Successful principals work to avoid "managing" crises—they do everything within their power to "prevent" crises! Granted, the challenges of violence in schools today has increased significantly. However, outside sources such as the Department of Homeland Security provide targeted violence prevention plans and other operational and model guides for aiding principals and teams in developing safety standards and measures.

Successful principals are always mindful of all students—notably, students of color. In far too many instances, students of color and poverty have long been ignored in schools across the nation. The most effective principals recognize how substantial change is essential—if not critical—to best ensuring the academic, behavioral, and social success of the nation's most at-risk populations. Daily, successful principals understand that the all too similar, status quo, and dated methods of instructional delivery require different, research-based, student-centered, and best-practice outcomes.

DISCUSSION QUESTIONS

1. Why are weekly (Monday morning, for example) meetings essential to better ensuring student, faculty, and staff success? Explain the purpose of such meetings.
2. Successful principals are always "checking the pulse" of the campus. What does this mean? Provide examples of how a principal must gauge campus teaching, learning, and leading.
3. What are characteristics of principal mindfulness? Why is mindfulness an important aspect of successful principal leadership? Provide detailed examples.
4. The best principals develop an open culture, positive climate, SMART goals and objectives (see page 58), and they are honest, ethical, moral, and transparent. How do these descriptors better ensure that campus leadership anticipates, adjusts, and learns?
5. What is the purpose of school-site academic coaches? How do these individuals instructionally assist school leaders and personnel? How do they aid in adjusting for everyday events?
6. Successful principals do more than manage. They anticipate and prevent. How so relative to school crises? Review Table 4.2: A Step-by-Step Violence Prevention Plan (see page 61). Of the seven steps identified, which one is essential to preventing a crisis? Explain why.
7. Examine Table 4.3: The Other Perspective: Students and Arrest/Referral Statistics. What must be learned from the table and by principals and prospective principals relative to this chapter section? Detail a reasoned response.

Table 4.3 The Other Perspective: Students and Arrest/Referral Statistics

Students	Overall Enrollment	Arrested	Referred to Law
Black	15.5%	33.4%	25.8%
Hispanic	24.7%	24.9%	22.5%
White	50.3%	33.7%	38.2%

CASE STUDY APPLICATION—STRANGERS, A TRUE STORY OF PRINCIPAL LEADERSHIP: ANTICIPATING, ADAPTING, ADJUSTING, AND LEARNING!

A few years ago, the fortitude of a school principal was tested. Realize that anticipating, adjusting, adapting, and learning are daily leadership qualities rarely addressed in the research literature. Many in the general public fail to recognize that hardly a day goes by that a principal doesn't face a challenge or crisis that demands adjusting and adapting. Successful principals learn to do more—they recognize the significance of anticipating.

Dr. Bosque Zavala, principal at Miegz Rhodes School, realized something had to give—something had to be made right! Far too long, the issue had been either audaciously overlooked or purposefully side-stepped. One way or another, it was now time for students to be placed first. Someone had to rectify a situation that some adults would find, inexplicably acceptable.

The students at Miegz Rhodes School had long been ignored. In fact, worse than ignored, these students of color and poverty had been segregated. Now, this can't be true, not today, not even a decade ago, let alone 30 or 50 years ago! Well, in fact, it wasn't so long ago that this true story occurred. Incredulous is the predictable response. The question: How and why? Simply accept the fact that it's a long story and somehow, someway, the noted segregation was actually legal. Yes, legal, but not ethical, certainly not moral. Now, returning to the main point of the story, principled leadership: anticipating, adjusting, adapting, and learning.

After several months of behind the scenes work, Dr. Zavala and three other district officials, working in tandem with the superintendent of schools, developed a plan to integrate the students of color and poverty with the other students in the school system. In many respects, it was a simple plan. Operate in a school no longer in use, create a new instructional setting that combined students from differing schools in the district into a single setting, and thus, bring students of color and poverty into the same building with white students of privilege and means.

Not a difficult proposition. However, there are people in this world who don't really care for such an idea. Now, recognize the story being shared is not something unknown and/or misunderstood. Watch the television news and sadly, there are way too many people in this great country who remain bigoted, even racist. While it may be difficult to differentiate the two terms, to spend time doing so overlooks the magnitude of this story: (1) students, equity, and equality; and (2) principals, anticipating, adjusting, adapting, and learning. And remember, "truth is stranger than fiction."

Principal Zavala, collaborating with the district office team, met one Tuesday night for a district-wide community forum to unveil the proposed plan with the intention of making a wrong a right. Anticipating that word would spread across the community regarding the proposed plan, preparation and associated adjustments had been made.

The night of the community meeting, at a centralized location in a school gymnasium that was filled to capacity, Dr. Zavala, the three district office administrators, and the superintendent entered the cavernous facility to a disruptive rumbling of dissatisfaction that moved across an audience of "concerned citizens." The local media came to attention. Cameras flashed. Video recorders buzzed. It was an imposing sight—one that Principal Zavala and accompanying administrative team had anticipated.

The evening unfolded, and not politely. Disgruntled stakeholders spoke, hecklers challenged, and "concerned citizens" sat with scowls on their faces and arms crossed in apparent disgust. At one point, after Dr. Zavala and the district team had spoken and community members and stakeholders had vented, the floor was open for questions. What unfolded were fewer questions but more venting. There was one statement from a parent who resided on the proverbial "right-side-of-the-tracks." The parent, using a microphone for effect, said: "I don't want my child mixing with those strangers!"

Principal Zavala, readily heckled, adjusted his response. Rather than speak in an angered tone, which came naturally considering the situation, he carefully crafted a calm response. He explained that his students were anything but strangers. He noted they were students, human beings in fact, who deserved an equitable opportunity and equal education as those children of the lady who had offered the egregious statement. Boos and more heckling ensued. Dr. Zavala adapted to the circumstances, held his ground, spoke more evenly and steadily, with compassion, and he actually quoted biblical principles. Dr. Zavala also shared stories of challenges his students faced on a daily basis.

Sadly, yet not unexpectedly, the crowd became anything but moved. At this point, the crowd grew louder. One agitator grabbed the microphone and shouted: "We've got rights and you can't make us do what we don't want to do! We can have your job! In fact, do us a favor, Zavala—resign tonight!"

The evening, as menacing as described, exemplifies an occasion when many school leaders would find it far easier to adapt to a community of bullies and allow a highly charged environment—with a continuous clamoring of "concerned citizens"—to take control by means of selfish temperaments, ungraciously bad behaviors, and attitudes of indifference. The "concerned citizens" were absolutely intent on denouncing the proposed plan designed to serve the educational and social needs of school children.

This could very well have been the right time for Principal Zavala to choose to adjust to the challenges presented and adopt an easy, if not cowardly, exit by stepping aside, asking the superintendent of schools to accept the crowd-incensed, viperous verdict, and therefore, dismiss the meeting and any suggestion of rectifying a moral impediment.

Principled Leadership Actions

The successful principal:

- Creates and initiates a campus vision and mission.
- Encourages and acknowledges the expertise and successes of others through high expectations.
- Inspires and empowers others to become leaders and risk-takers.
- Collaborates and facilitates leading, teaching, and learning.
- Expresses ideas and strong ideals.
- Communicates with clarity, in a concise manner.
- Chooses words carefully and skillfully.
- Organizes ideas effectively in written and verbal communiques.
- Exhibits long-term commitments to students.
- Creates a supportive learning environment.
- Understands the learning community and stakeholders, holding all accountable.
- Creates an open, student-centered culture and positive climate.
- Establishes high expectations through strong curricular goals and student-focused objectives.
- Demonstrates a dedication to academic excellence and achievement for all students.
- Pursues equity and justice for all students.
- Makes decisions that are timely, relevant, and well-conceived.
- Makes decisions that reflect use of sound judgment and common sense.
- Analyzes opposing points of view. Works to develop appropriate and measured responses.
- Respects others and practices confidentiality.
- Demonstrates organizational stability, ability, time management, and tasks prioritization.
- Exercises authority appropriately.
- Follows established laws, codes, policies, regulations, and procedures.

Application Questions

1. Connolly (2008) suggests principals must anticipate situations whereby they have the courage to exercise their convictions. Explain how Dr. Bosque Zavala did so as revealed in the case study? Which of the bulleted principled leadership actions apply?
2. Principals, on a daily basis, face high-maintenance parents, out-of-control students, and "concerned citizens" who state they value education

but obviously not enough to support and respect the judgment and professionalism of teachers and administrators. How must a principal, like Dr. Zavala, anticipate such situations and then, adjust and advance an instructional vision—notably, when readily and regularly attacked? Relate your answer to the bulleted principled leadership actions.

3. Principals must realize they cannot win every battle. However, effective leader anticipation must dictate that principals never run away from such battles. It is no easy task to face resentment in the field of administrative practice. Think of a situation where a principal handled the resentment of a disgruntled employee, the wrath of an irrational parent, or the rage of a disruptive and disrespectful student. What's a principal to do? Offer a written response to the actions of anticipating, adjusting, and learning, and then relate answers to the listing of principled leadership actions.
4. Principals live in the advent of social media whereby a greater risk of character assassination can come from parents, students, and even teachers. A single, disgruntled individual can instantly damage or destroy the reputation of a principal with a false accusation. How are principals to anticipate, adjust, and react to persevere actions, and even survive in the face of real digital accusations or face-to-face threats? Which of the principled leadership actions apply?
5. Place yourself in the role of Dr. Zavala, the district leadership team, and superintendent, as described in the case study. Can the situation be resolved to best benefit the students? What principled actions of anticipation and adjustment relate and how should the situation be addressed/solved? Be specific and begin the written response with "Now, for the rest of the story…"
6. Finally, reflect and think of an occasion whereby you witnessed, firsthand, the anticipatory and adjusting actions of a school leader. Detail this account and share with your peers or colleagues.
7. What can a principal or prospective principal learn from this case study? Provide a specific and/or detailed answer.

AFTERTHOUGHT

Be ever-mindful, always alert, stand firm, stay strong, and be prepared in anticipation, for the door to effective principled leadership and service may be opened to you. And while there are many challenges, be steadfast, committed, dedicated, and always allow for adjustments to better thrive in the principal leadership environment. Know that anticipatory deeds, and associated adjustments exhibited, must never be in vain. On a daily basis, remember, students must always come first!

Chapter 5

Daily Step #5

Recognize, Understand, and Embrace Diversity

"One of the most important factors that impedes effective leadership is bias!" —Ann Morrison, Randall White, and Ellen Van Velsor (*Breaking the Glass Ceiling*)

"We need to help students and parents cherish and preserve the ethnic and cultural diversity that nourishes and strengthens this community—and this nation!" —Cesar Chavez (*Education of the Heart—Cesar Chavez in His Own Words*)

WHAT DO YOU BRING TO THE TABLE?

Educators have a variety of reasons for entering into administrative positions. There are personal and professional reasons. For some, it's a noble pursuit. For others, it's because they wish to serve. Many see it as a next step after classroom teaching, sort of a natural career progression. Still more pursue the principal position for financial reasons. There are some who tire of the classroom and want a change, while others gravitate to the administrative role mistakenly believing it is an easier job.

Some educators are targeted for leadership, some are mentored throughout their career while others will set their own career agenda. Experiences within the school, interactions with students and colleagues, and extracurricular activities are other examples that play an important part in whether an educator will consider pursuing the principalship. For whatever reason, potential principals must explore their own ideology and educational values and beliefs.

Successful principals truly unpack their story, and their reasons for why they pursue the principalship. (Recall, chapter 1 briefly touched upon the journey of new principals.) Each individual brings unique experiences to the role. Each has a special story to share. Many refer to a career in education, in the principalship specifically, as a "calling"—much like that of a minister, priest, or rabbi. These stories, each experience, includes upbringing, incidents in schools, familial relationships, and the list goes on and on. But there will always be biases and certain held beliefs that, in fairness, must be addressed.

UNCONSCIOUS OR IMPLICIT BIAS

One of the most important aspects of self-reflection is to understand the unconscious or implicit biases that are embedded individually and, certainly, within society (Banks, Eberhardt & Ross, 2006). Research has long revealed that every individual possesses unconscious, if not implicit, assumptions that serve to influence judgements and perceptions of self and others (Handelsman & Sakraney, 2015). Implicit bias encompasses subconscious feelings, perceptions, attitudes, and even stereotypes that have formed resulting from previous stimuli and encouragements. Implicit bias is based on numerous individual aspects, to include but not limited to, an individual's: (1) gender; (2) age; (3) race; and (4) ethnicity.

However, implicit bias isn't only about people. School principals and personnel also have implicit biases that can influence their practices. For example, many schools adhere to certain policies and practices that, in fact, serve as disadvantages to certain school community members, such as calling a faculty meeting when faculty parents need to be picking up their children at day care, which does in actuality discriminate against faculty with young children.

Bias at school may not seem to be deliberate—schedules, for example, were often developed during a long-ago era when most faculty were men who were married to women who did not work outside the home, and stayed at home to care for the children. Today, successful school leaders consider how past biases and current lack of awareness can make a school unfriendly in actions and appearances to faculty and students, notably of certain demographic groups (Handelsman & Sakraney, 2015).

Unconscious, implicit, and institutional bias are also school-related issues. Principals must be aware of societal implications of bias within a school, classroom, and even attributed to school personnel. The following types of bias and definitions are derived from the U.S. Department of Justice's *Community Relations Services Toolkit for Policing* (n. d.) at www.justice.gov/crs/file/836431/download. While the Department of Justice toolkit is actually geared toward police, the description of the types of biases are relevant. Summarized in Table 5.1 are the different types of biases.

Table 5.1 Types of Bias

Type of Bias (Actual or Perceived)	Definition
Race, Color, National Origin, & Ethnicity	*Racial discrimination* is treating a person adversely due to that individual's race or characteristics associated with that race, such as hair texture or facial features. *Color discrimination* is discriminating against people due to the color of their skin. *National origin* discrimination involves treating people unfavorably due to where they are from or their ethnicity or accent.
Sex, Gender, Gender Identity, & Sexual Orientation	*Sex* refers to a person's biological status and is typically categorized as male, female, or intersex. *Gender* refers to the attitudes, feelings, and behaviors that a given culture associates with a person's biological sex. *Gender identity* refers to one's sense of self as male, female, or transgender. *Sexual orientation* refers to the sex of those to whom a person is sexually and romantically attracted.
Religion	Some laws protect people against *religious discrimination* in certain ways, such as employment. It is important to understand basic tenets of major religions. For example, a culture or religion may avoid eye contact. It may appear to be a sign of deceit or evasion, but some cultures dictate this as a sign of modesty.
Disability	Protected under the Americans with Disabilities Act (ADA). When interacting with *individuals with disabilities*, it is important to be aware of various types of physical and mental impairments covered under the law, including vision and hearing impairments and conditions such as epilepsy or Autism Spectrum Disorder. Often, these impairments can interfere with a person's ability to hear, see, understand, or respond to questions, directions, or orders.

SUCCESSFUL PRINCIPALS AND IMPLICIT BIAS

Successful principals are familiar with unconscious or implicit bias as well as institutional bias. It is not good enough to think or believe that one isn't biased. One principal related a story of working as a teacher in a school with a large population of Blacks, Asians, and other marginalized groups:

> As a minority myself, I noticed that many of the older teachers would make jokes about some of the students of color. What on the surface may have appeared harmless, actually played on the stereotypes of the students, calling one hallway the "curry corner." Many of these teachers had been working with the same groups of students for so long, that they had begun only seeing the negative aspects of these students—poverty, stereotypes, and religious differences. But worst of all was that these stereotypes became their normal views of these marginalized students. (Mungal, 2019)

Principals must address biases directly, always bringing this conversation to the forefront of teacher-principal discussions.

Principals must collect school and district data on discipline, suspensions, and length of punishments. Successful principals carefully and thoughtfully examine such data. Successful principals compare this data to other schools and districts with similar demographics to better compare school norms, values, beliefs, biases, and the effect on disciplinary actions. Principals must understand the impact of bias and how it actually plays out within a school. Successful principals learn from data to best inform the learning community as to how implicit bias impacts students, parents, faculty, staff, and community members!

ADDRESSING BIAS

Principals must be aware of different types of bias that occur within schools. Implicit bias is all about the existence and persistence of societal inequities, not just at school but also in the criminal justice system, in the healthcare industry, and even in employment (Staats, 2015). The Law Society identifies several types of biases that are predominant within workplaces that principals can examine as related to their practice. For example, successful principals review their recruiting and selection practices so they can be made more neutral by removing name, age, and gender from applications (Thompson, 2018).

Many schools, private and public, have published steps to reduce bias in the workplace. Principals can use professional development time to ensure teachers and staff address biases. Online questionnaires exist, such as Project Implicit (2011) from Harvard University at implicit.harvard.edu/implicit/takeatest.html. Project Implicit has 14 different tests on Religion, Disability, Skin-tone, Gender-Science, Sexuality, and various other questionnaires on ethnicity. Google re:Work (2019) also explores how decisions are made at work at their website rework.withgoogle.com/subjects/unbiasing/. Microsoft (2015) also offers an e-Lesson on Unconscious Bias at www.mslearning.microsoft.com/course/72169/launch.

Principals must address and eliminate workplace bias. Summarized below are eight recommendations for principals to follow based on research by Blackman, 2018; Fiarman, 2016; Bennett, 2019; Suttie, 2016; Castro, 2017; Perez-Isiah, 2018; and Thompson, 2018.

1. *Increase Self Awareness*—Administrators must recognize the intersections of race, ethnicity, gender, sexual orientation, religion, and socioeconomic status. Principals and teams must recognize how personal

identification within a particular group enables privilege. Principals must actively listen to marginalized groups whose life experiences have been uniquely different. Principals must learn to become an advocate for marginalized groups and become aware of personal biases and, thus, question how decision-making affects problem-solving.

2. *Develop Professional Development to Increase Workplace Awareness*—Principals must openly encourage discussions about bias with faculty and staff, normalizing conversations about bias by incorporating direct teaching and modeling techniques which openly and honestly identify bias. Principals can use professional development sessions to focus on culturally relevant pedagogies, diversity, and multiculturalism. Principals must offer training to faculty and staff so they better understand implicit or unconscious bias and help team members to develop strategies to address biases. Such strategies must address generalizations, challenge decision-making processes, include online self-testing, reduce biased group-thinking, and challenge personal zones of comfort.
3. *Naming or Tackling Bias*—Increasing awareness means trusting colleagues to provide honest views. Fiarman (2016) cites Singleton and Linton's 2006 model regarding four means of courageous conversation: 1) stay engaged; 2) expect to experience discomfort; 3) speak truthfully; and 4) expect and accept a lack of closure.
4. *Interact with Diverse Community Groups*—Principals must seek and connect with diverse groups. Such interactions lead to a decrease in stress, prejudice, and views on social hierarchy. Developing such relationships aid in tearing down the barriers of prejudice. Principals and teams must find methods to learn about and better interact with racial and ethnic groups.
5. *Increase Empathy*—Replacing undesirable associations with positive connections is a way a principal can counteract unconscious bias. Teachers who do not come from or live within the communities where their students live have difficulty understanding their students' life experiences which often result in harsher student treatment. Principals and teams must also confront old personal and negative biases with new and positive perspectives.
6. *Utilize Data*—As a means of holding principals and teams accountable. Data will enable a principal to discern patterns within race, gender, and socioeconomic status and biases among teachers. Successful principals analyze data on suspensions, and, most important, share said data with teachers and staff.
7. *Reject Colorblindness*—Colorblindness avoids and certainly minimizes lived experiences. Colorblindness refers to the belief that people do not see race or color and, thus, recognize all people as being the same.

Colorblindness, in a positive reality and sense, aids individuals in avoiding negativity associated with diversity, race, and culture. Being colorblind therefore suppresses those learned negative views that perpetuate systemic racism. Failing to see color means failing to acknowledge the current system of injustice for marginalized groups.
8. *Revise and Revisit Bias*—Addressing implicit bias is a constant battle. Principals must consistently revisit biases and challenge the belief system of self and others. Principals must regularly revisit data to hold everyone accountable. Successful principals constantly address implicit bias to ensure that teachers never slide back into old stereotypical beliefs.

THE PRINCIPALSHIP AND MARGINALIZED GROUPS

Successful principals uplift groups who remain in the margins—groups, for example, such as LGBQTIA, people of color, and different cultures. The very best principals ensure a culture of equity. Successful principals unpack their biases and push against common narratives that perpetuate inequities. These leaders are aware of the roadblocks that regularly remain in place preventing marginalized groups from opportunities to promote and succeed.

Culturally relevant pedagogy seeks to connect the home and community experiences of the students to school culture (Ladson-Billings, 1995; Mungal, 2020b). Schools tend to be based on a system of coursework and, at times, instructional meritocracy. Tied into the notion of implicit bias, culturally relevant pedagogy can counteract the biases and stereotypes of teachers and administrators.

To implement culturally relevant pedagogies in the classroom, successful principals ensure that teachers establish inclusion, develop positive attitudes, enhance meaningful relationships with students who are perceived as different, and foster, in *all* of their students, a high level of confidence (Guido, 2017). Successful principals must be prepared to embrace and promote different cultures, push against teacher and institutional biases, and teach and use creative delivery methods to engage students.

To be successful with culturally responsive pedagogy strategies, principals must ensure that teachers do the following (1) Engage and learn about students' life stories; (2) Integrate applicable word problems with students' stories; (3) Relate new concepts by connecting to students' interests; (4) Invite guests of various cultures, ethnicities, and perceived differences to the classroom; (5) Utilize various forms of delivery for content (articles/puzzles/games/brief lectures); (6) Call on all students to share their experiences, not just the ones who always answer; (7) Include relevant media (books, movies, news); (8) Support in-class study time; (9) Encourage students to create their own projects; (10) Support peer teaching; and (11) Involve parents by frequent connections and interactions (Guido, 2017).

There are numerous national websites that examine and recommend strategies. The National Association of Secondary School Principals (NASSP) (2019) has a position statement on Culturally Responsive Schools at www.nassp.org/policy-advocacy-center/nassp-position-statements/culturally-responsive-schools/. The National Association of Elementary School Principals (NAESP) (2018) shares several free publications such as The Principal's Guide to Building Culturally Responsive Schools at www.naesp.org/principal-s-guide-building-culturally-responsive-schools. There are also state-wide colleges and universities that also provide useful strategies such as Culturally Responsive Education: A Primer for Policy and Practice from New York University at steinhardt.nyu.edu/scmsAdmin/media/users/emj309/CRE_Primer.pdf, or Brown University's The Teaching Alliance (2019) Culturally Responsive Teaching at www.brown.edu/academics/education-alliance/teaching-diverse-learners/strategies-0/culturally-responsive-teaching-0. Consider a quick online search to find local or state institutes of higher education for culturally relevant pedagogies.

COMMUNICATION: A KEY TO A SUCCESSFUL PRINCIPALSHIP

A key component of principal leadership is the ability to effectively communicate initiatives, policies, and school and district visions. The National School Public Relations Association, (n.d.), identifies 10 communication strategies for principal success:

1. *Communicate Early and Often*—Quickly dispel misconceptions about quality and the safety of schools. In crisis situations, it is vital to communicate immediately with students, faculty, staff, parents, and the public. Principals must be prepared to deliver the message by multiple means and in multiple formats to reach differing audiences.
2. *Communicate Face-to-Face as Often as Possible*—One-to-one communication is the most effective method followed by small group discussions or meetings. Ensure that students are also informed as they are the most vital aspect of any crisis, and certainly, any normal situation.
3. *Develop Relations with All Members of the Learning Community*—Involve the learning community in developing solutions. Connect with and gather information from leaders within the community. Ensure that they are included in communications.

4. *Utilize Staff as Ambassadors*—Establish protocols for faculty and staff to know when they are to interact with community members. This is especially true for support staff who tend to come from the local community.
5. *Create Exemplary Customer Service*—For all visitors, ensure that administrators, office staff, and faculty extend courteous welcomes such as: "Hello" or "How are you?" and always issue a friendly "goodbye." Goodwill builds strong bonds with community members.

    Remember, while customer service is quickly becoming a "norm of the past" in places like grocery, department, and big-box stores, consistently warm and personal greetings must remain the standard in all schools and must be exhibited by all personnel. Today, in many instances, customer service must be taught. It may seem trivial, but it is true! Younger generations of school faculty and staff and even administrators have not grown up in a service-friendly environment. A simple "good morning or afternoon" is fine, but not sufficient. This greeting must be followed up by the next sentence: "How can I help you?"
6. *Help Parents Understand their Important Role in the Education Process*—Successful principals help support parents in becoming more involved in their children's education. Reading to children, being seen reading, setting academic, behavioral, and social examples, and showing an interest in school work are just a few ways parents can support schools. Principals, administrative team members, and faculty and staff must provide support and training to better assist parents in understanding how important and influential a parent is to a child's education. Principals must set an example for all personnel to observe by welcoming parents into the school family.
7. *Be Brief and to the Point*—Keeping messages short and simple will allow all audiences to better receive and understand the information. Avoid educational jargon and acronyms. Recently, a school memo home to parents read: "PTO members plan to meet in the MPR across from the IRC and just down the hall from the CLC." Brief, yes. To the point, certainly. But what was the message? Successful principals plan their content and practice their delivery.
8. *Never Lie*—If you don't know the answer, say you don't know and that you will get back to the person with an answer. Be sure to follow up and never speculate.
9. *Do a Better than Good Job*—Maintain communication with partners. Be honest in all communications and address issues as promptly as possible.
10. *Develop a Communications Plan*—Determine the audience, how information is to be disseminated, where information will be gathered, and plan to meet such needs. Involve faculty and staff in ensuring the messages are being disseminated. Review, revise, and update communication plans regularly.

To ensure effective communication, successful principals and staff must be available to students, faculty, staff, parents, and community members. Successful principals must be aware of what is occurring at the school-site level, seek out faculty, staff, students, parents, and community members and listen to and understand their views. This means dedicating time to meet, and then asking follow-up questions to best clarify information.

* * *

JUAN'S STORY: "YO HABLO ESPAÑOL?"

A superintendent from a southwest border city related a powerful story of his interaction with a principal on his very first day of school as a teen. This superintendent grew up in poverty and had emigrated to the United States from a small town in Mexico. The story:

> I went to live with my father, his wife, and his children in Whittier, California. What a culture shock! To make matters worse, I did not speak English. I arrived in Whittier just a few days before the beginning of the school year. One of my half-brothers attended California High School and my other brother attended La Serna High School. On the first day of school, my father drove us to La Serna High School. When we arrived, he simply dropped us off in front of the school. He did not bother to escort me in for registration. I assumed my father expected my brother to help me, which did not happen.
>
> I got out of the car and walked towards the school, practically trembling with fear and insecurity. My brother went to his classes with his friends. I sat on a bench waiting for him to return. I was confused, not knowing what to do, where to go, or who to talk to. I did not speak English and I did not know anyone. I avoided eye contact with everyone who passed by. I had never felt so lonely and helpless.
>
> Approximately twenty minutes had passed when I looked up and panicked when I saw a tall White man walking towards me. When he arrived where I was sitting, he shook my hand, smiled, and said something in English. I did not understand what he said, of course, and I simply uttered the words: "No English." He replied in Spanish gently offering: "Yo hablo Español?" I do not remember what else he said, but I never forgot what he did.
>
> Then, he took me to the office, registered me, walked me around the school, welcomed me to the campus and took me to my first science class with Ms. Evans. At lunchtime, I met with my brother in the school cafeteria. When I saw the man who registered me standing by one of the lunch lines, I asked my brother who he was. "The principal," he replied. My first instinct was to go and thank him, but I was too embarrassed to say anything. (Martinez, 2017).

Successful principals make a difference by knowing the demographics of a school and of a community. The very best principals use this knowledge to become effective communicators—all for the benefit of students.

Take Time to Think and Reflect

1. Of the 10 communication strategies for principal success, which *one* most relates to this scenario? Explain why.
2. Of the nine remaining communication strategies for principal success, which ones exemplify the actions of the principal at La Serna High School in Whittier, California, as identified in this scenario.
3. Explain by what means the student in the scenario is considered a member of a marginalized group. How should a principal and faculty, today, reach out to a student as has been described in this true-life account—beyond effective communication strategies?

SUCCESSFUL PRINCIPALS ENCOURAGE ALTERNATIVE VIEWS AND EMBRACE OPPOSING VIEWS

Principals are sometimes viewed as solitary decision-makers who bear the brunt of leadership. Now, halfway through the text, the reader recognizes the importance of outstanding school leadership—what makes for a successful principal. It is essential to once again revisit principal leadership from a decision-making perspective, notably in the context of understanding opposing views.

People are frequently hesitant to introduce new, differing, or even opposing information if they feel uncomfortable or not valued. Many individuals prefer to play up good news and suppress bad news. Instead of encouraging and rewarding opposing views, some principals are apt, as is human nature, to focus on the good when opposing information, data, and/or research actually confirms what is a transparent truth. This approach to leading, ignoring the truth, good or bad, is corollary to a horse fitted with blinkers or blinders. Such an approach to leadership provides a very small window or perspective into reality. Important note: Principals and teams can never change what they choose not to see!

Encouraging alternate views or embracing opposing views must be a school-site norm. Personnel who fail to speak up about important issues are often reluctant to voice good ideas for fear the new notions may bring about negative consequences to themselves This reluctance can also relate to a fear that a superior will not appreciate the idea because it is different or it may actually criticize the status quo. Successful principals always address personnel reluctance to speak up, encouraging them to speak out, and speak truthfully.

Successful principals assemble leadership teams that embrace the shared vision of members of the learning community. This is an important component for ensuring that there is a smooth and unified front to promote not only a strong, student-centered vision but high expectations which can be embraced by everyone to best benefit student achievement. Principals who are surrounded by "yes-people" commit a terrible disservice to the entire learning community. Opposing viewpoints and ideas, when student-focused and instructionally sound, better ensure exceptional decision-making and problem-solving.

Successful principals understand that every vision and accompanying plan will come with opposing perspectives, certain challenges, issues and problems, and often with unintended consequences. Successful principals acknowledge opposing views. Opposing views must be approached as outside-the-box thinking. In fact, successful principals encourage leadership teams and personnel to be critical, from a healthy point of view, of campus initiatives. Principals that allow for the critiquing of initiatives in many respects are developing a system of anticipating potential problems. This approach to school leadership can very well lead to a more thorough understanding of the potential issues and thus, encounter issues before they become serious problems.

Successful principals always welcome alternative and opposing views. Successful principals build in critique and critical thinking as part of campus leadership training. Such training includes the opportunity for personnel to express opposing views. Successful principals accept opposing views as pertinent to the decision-making process. Critique must always be supported and encouraged. Individuals with opposing views must feel comfortable to express themselves. Successful principals recognize that dissenting views serve as opportunities to collect information and perspectives, and thus, to learn. Allowing stakeholders the opportunity to express themselves and their concerns will bring forward different ideas and better approaches to decision-making and problem-solving.

NEVER "NO" BUT "LET'S ARRANGE TO MEET"

Principals are consistently bombarded by various demands on their time. Much of a principal's time is structured around the planned daily schedule of meetings, paperwork, emails, telephone calls, and visibility on the campus. Successful principals use visibility to connect with students, parents, and school personnel. This means stakeholders can easily and readily monopolize a principal's time. At times, personnel will want to engage a principal immediately. Successful principals ensure that there is time set aside to meet with stakeholders.

Successful principals work diligently to never say "no" when stakeholders want to talk, but will attempt to arrange a time to meet with students, parents, or school personnel. Successful principals make every effort to ensure that individuals feel acknowledged, welcomed, and that concerns are valued and addressed. Successful principals take time to actively listen and respond to individual concerns.

Successful principals instruct office staff to ensure that they are accommodating parents, students, and teachers. Office staff must be cognizant of the times that stakeholders are available to meet with the principal. Parents may not be available to meet during regular school hours, and successful principals and teams work with parents who face challenges with jobs and finding time to meet.

Successful principals also encourage connecting with stakeholders via telephone or email as a means of helping parents. Successful principals have office staff follow up with parents to ensure that their voices are heard and their issues are addressed. This process must be a daily process whereby parents and other stakeholders recognize that a principal or team member will reply within a 24-hour period. Within an eight-hour period is even better! No one appreciates waiting, especially when a concern needs addressing! Remember, successful principals never say "no" to a meeting with a stakeholder. The very best principals state: "Let's arrange to meet," and then do so!

SUCCESSFUL PRINCIPALS EMBRACE DIVERSE PERSONALITIES AND PERSPECTIVES

Every school is a microcosm of society. As initially mentioned in chapter 3, school personnel include administrators, specialists, support staff, students, and teachers. Personnel represent different ages, maturities, ethnicities, nationalities, and abilities. They bring their own issues and attitudes to a school. This mix can introduce volatility one day and grace the next. Diversity introduces a myriad of personalities that school leaders must address. Recall the words of William Sloane Coffin, American clergyman and longtime peace activist: "Diversity maybe the hardest thing for a society to live with, and perhaps the most dangerous thing for a society to be without" (AZ Quotes, 2015a)!

Successful principals work to learn, understand, and embrace diverse campus personalities. Some diversity includes certain teachers with difficult reputations, teachers who may not be as engaged as others, or as they once were, or teachers who have simply burned out.

Issues with teachers will eventually come to the attention of a school leader. Such problems may arrive at a principal's desk, so to speak, through either official or unofficial channels. The official channels may be via written correspondence or verbal complaints regarding problems that teachers are experiencing or from indirect word of mouth from teachers, students, or parents. It is important that principals do due diligence to uncover details and, most importantly, to ensure that there aren't internal or external factors that are creating a toxic environment.

Difficult teachers can have a negative effect on students, colleagues, and principals! A quick fix is always the transfer of the teacher to another school, but that just makes the teacher the next principal's problem. However, in some cases a fresh start may be best for all stakeholders. Nevertheless, a principal must always arrange to meet with a difficult teacher to better understand and address the situation, long before a transfer is contemplated.

Meeting with difficult teachers with an open mind can aid a principal in finding a solution to a problem. Successful principals are open-minded and *actively listen*. Glasser's Reality Therapy can also be beneficial to connecting with difficult teachers. Glasser's Reality Therapy emphasizes problem-solving and decision-making to better gain positive results (Arnold, 2015).

HOW TO WORK WITH DIFFICULT TEACHERS

Successful principals establish trust with difficult teachers so these teachers understand that the principal wants to be part of the solution, not the problem. Yet, this can be a struggle if the principal is perceived to be part of the problem. In such cases, it is easy for a principal to become adversarial. Therefore, principals may recommend that the difficult teacher discuss the issue with someone on the leadership team with whom the teacher is more trusting and comfortable.

Principals must always be transparent, especially with difficult teachers. Transparency is a critical key when it comes to developing trust. Successful principals engage difficult teachers by not only being transparent but also by showing respect, concern, and establishing a high level of trust. A transparent, respectful, and trusting environment, as well as a willingness to listen will go a long way to solving problems for all teachers.

Difficult teachers can also include teachers who have been in the classroom for a significant period of time. Sometimes, these teachers may not feel valued; their voices—they sense—are no longer being heard. Thus, these teachers are historically critical of district and principal initiatives and of notably younger teacher colleagues who they perceive to be more acceptable to change.

Difficult teachers are frequently dissenters simply because they are fearful—fearful of change, fearful of the transformation from the comforts of the status quo to new and different instructional approaches. Successful principals work to establish a connection with these difficult teachers. The best principals focus on the strengths and interests of difficult teachers, value their experiences, and engage their knowledge and expertise as a means of showing trust, confidence, and concern.

Successful principals and the leadership teams meet with teachers who feel they are not valued, or teachers who are critical, or teachers who have burned out. Finding ways to either engage difficult teachers or offer support to these teachers will ultimately pay dividends.

McEwan (2005) offers 20 recommendations for working with difficult teachers, to include: (1) treating them with dignity and respect; (2) avoiding humiliating or threatening them in private or public; (3) providing explicit and honest feedback; (4) providing clear and direct expectations; (5) avoiding using the silent treatment or attempted isolation; (6) ensuring a student-first and -centered instructional focus; (7) exuding defensive posturing; (8) avoiding aggressive or hostile behaviors; (9) nurturing an open culture and positive climate; (10) conducting assertive interventions; (11) dealing directly with the problem; (12) avoiding jumping to conclusions; (13) providing clear and explicit details, information, and reasons for instructional changes; (14) being fair, yet always firm; (15) admitting mistakes and sincerely apologizing when in the wrong; (16) being open to all ideas and considerations; (17) valuing the personal as well as professional well-being of others; (18) being assertive, because pushover principals seldom are able to work with difficult teachers; (19) building character by displaying character; and (20) documenting factually all difficult teachers whose actions, discussions, and confrontations are disruptive or insubordinate.

Interestingly enough, students who are sometimes uninspired, lacking motivation or interest, even difficult themselves, or are simply attempting to find their own way, often gravitate toward difficult teachers, especially if the students feel that such teachers are supportive or allies. Successful principals utilize difficult teachers to appeal to these students by having them start student-centered clubs or activities that interest both the teacher and students.

Bottom line: There are difficult teachers on every school staff! They may not fit into what is expected of teachers, but they can serve as positive influences on students. As noted above, principal influence and guidance is the key! Principals who regularly meet with difficult teachers gain insight into their goals for teaching.

Successful principals ensure that students are protected from certain teachers, difficult or not. There are times when listening and being transparent and supportive fail. No amount of professional development or engaging certain teachers will always be successful. However, the very best principals limit the negative impact of difficult teachers. Successful principals support and are visible and available to students who may have to interact with a negative or difficult teacher. Successful principals ensure that students are receiving support within the classroom of a difficult teacher and also offer students an outlet to engage the school principal if and when problems become untenable.

Finally, always remember: Successful principals make daily straightforward decisions when working with difficult teachers. The inappropriate actions of difficult teachers must be documented. Principals must, at the same time, offer problematic teachers support and recommend support, if necessary, from the school district. Difficult, problematic, or disruptive teachers can certainly have a larger impact than just in the classroom. These teachers interact with colleagues, parents, community members, and other members of the administrative team. Successful principals always recognize the need to take effective, essential, and immediate attention and action!

FINAL THOUGHTS

Successful principals recognize that unconscious, implicit, and institutional bias are school-related issues. Types of bias include actual or perceived race, color, national origin, and ethnic discrimination as well as sex, gender, gender identity, and sexual orientation discrimination. Additionally, religious discrimination along with disability discrimination are regrettably, other forms of bias in schools. Principals must address biases directly, always bringing this conversation to the forefront of principal-teacher-student-parent-community member discussions.

Successful principals in discussions regarding bias increase self-awareness, develop professional development to increase work-place awareness, name and tackle bias, interact with diverse community groups, increase empathy, utilize data as a means of holding the learning community accountable, reject colorblindness, and revise and revisit bias.

Successful principals recognize and uplift marginalized groups to include those of the LGBQTIA community, people of color, as well as different cultures. The very best principals push against common narratives that perpetuate inequities. These principals engage and learn about students' lives outside of school; ensure the integration of word problems applicable to student life stories and related concepts that connect student interests to learning; invite guests of various cultures, ethnicities, and perceived differences to classrooms; call on students to share their life experiences; include relevant media as related to marginalized groups; and involve parents by making frequent connections and interactions.

Successful principals communicate early and often; frequently communicate face-to-face; develop relationships with all members of the learning community; utilize staff as community ambassadors; create exemplary customer service; and aid parents in understanding their vital role in the education of their children.

Successful principals encourage alternate views and embrace opposing views, serving as active listeners and always embracing diverse personalities and perspectives. The very best principals know how to work with difficult teachers earning their trust through transparency, honesty, and respectfulness.

Successful principals avoid humiliating or threatening others; provide explicit and honest feedback; provide clear and direct expectations; nurture an open culture and positive climate; deal directly with problems, avoid jumping to conclusions; admit mistakes; remain open to all ideas and considerations; are assertive, yet fair and firm; and document factually the actions of those who are disruptive or insubordinate.

DISCUSSION QUESTIONS

1. Consider the first section of the chapter, entitled "What Do You Bring to the Table?" Respond to the question: "What do you bring to the table" as a current or prospective school leader? What's your story or reason for pursuing the principalship?
2. Explain unconscious, implicit, and instructional bias. How does bias relate to school leadership and schooling in general? Have you personally observed or experienced bias in the workplace?
3. Which two of the eight "Addressing Bias" recommendations for principals to attend to and/or eliminate workplace bias do you perceive to be the most effective? Explain why.
4. Examine the eleven culturally responsive pedagogy strategies and explain which three would be most effective in successfully aiding marginalized groups in schools.
5. In the chapter section "Communication: A Key to a Successful Principalship," ten key communication strategies for principal success are identified. Consider a principal who exhibits exceptional communication skills and apply at least four of the ten strategies which would apply. Next, consider a principal with poor communication skills and determine which

four or more of the ten strategies would serve to improve said principal's communication skills.
6. Detail why successful principals encourage alternative views and embrace opposing views relative to school personnel.
7. McEwan (2005) offers 20 recommendations for principals who work with difficult teachers. Consider a difficult teacher you have encountered and which of the 20 recommendations would best serve to improve a principal-difficult teacher relationship?

CASE STUDY APPLICATION—WHAT ARE YOU DOING OR WHAT SHOULD YOU BE DOING?

Sunga Lumgan, principal at Ronotto School, walked quietly and somewhat dishearteningly from Wenda Rossenon's classroom. Wenda was perpetually difficult, to say the least. She was never pleased with anything Principal Lumgan said or did. For that matter, she was seldom pleased with anything anyone else said or did!

Wenda Rossenon was not a positive force on campus. She fashioned trouble when trouble need not be conceived or created. She disrupted faculty meetings with loud and boisterous behaviors. She intimidated both novice and experienced faculty. She lived to make members of the administrative team uncomfortable or even look foolish.

Principal Lumgan was at a loss. He shook his head, looked skyward, and said: "What am I to do?" As he continued to walk along the school's main hallway, he suddenly recalled, from days long past, a discussion on Glasser's Reality Therapy. He amusingly said to himself: "Why in the world am I thinking back to my own days in teacher training?"

At the time, one of his undergraduate university professors described how teachers who see students who are not on task, ask the students, "What are you doing?" The principal now recalled that this type of question only invited a student to respond by describing the wrongful behavior. Instead, the professor stated that Glasser's Reality Therapy recommends that a teacher ask, "What should you be doing?" This query is designed to ensure that a student will first recognize the inappropriate behavior, then identify the related consequence, and, finally, eliminate the unacceptable behavior.

"Interesting," reflected the principal. This type of question places the onus on the offender to correctly recognize the incorrect behavior and then to accept that there is a correct behavior to be followed.

Principal Lumgan inwardly smiled and thought to himself: "Yep, I think I can use Glasser's Reality Theory on Wenda Rossenon!" The principal mused: "It just might work. Shoot, it's worth a try!"

Application Questions

1. How might Principal Sunga Lumgan incorporate Glasser's Reality Theory in relation to Wenda Rossenon? Provide a situation and an example.
2. At the next faculty meeting, reality sits in. Wenda abruptly interrupts one of the academic coaches during an instructional presentation and rudely shouts out: "None of what you're saying makes sense. I don't see how any of it applies to us. What a waste of time!" Apply Glasser's Reality Theory and write an appropriate retort.
3. Explain how unconscious or implicit bias might play a role as detailed in this scenario. Re-examine Table 5.1 ("Types of Bias") as a means of determining if any of the four types of bias as defined apply to this scenario.
4. Examine the chapter section entitled "How to Work with Difficult Teachers," and explain which of the means identified might best relate to Principal Lumgan working with Wenda Rossenon.
5. Of McEwan's 20 recommendations, as previously noted in the chapter, for working with difficult teachers, which relate most readily to this scenario? Explain why.

Chapter 6

Daily Step #6

Meet, Greet, and Engage in Good Humor

"A sense of humor is part of the art of leadership, of getting along with people, of getting things done!" —Dwight D. Eisenhower, 34th president of the United States and supreme commander of Allied Forces in Europe, World War II (Brainy Quotes, 2001–2019a)

"Good humor is a tonic for mind and body. It is the best antidote for anxiety. It is a professional asset. It attracts and maintains friends. It lightens human burdens. It is the direct route to peace and contentment!" —Grenville Kleiser, author (AZ Quotes, 2015b)

DO THIS FIRST, EVERY DAY—SMILE!

Once popularized by singing artists such as Louis Armstrong, Dean Martin, Doris Day, Frank Sinatra, Ella Fitzgerald, and more recently, Michael Bublé, and included in a sixth-season episode of the comedy television show *Seinfeld*, the 1928 classic song *When You're Smiling* reminds the administrative leader that "when you're smiling, the whole world smiles with you" (Lyrics.com, 2001–2019). Noted below is research worth grinning about!

A smile begins in the sensory passages or corridors of the brain's anterior temporal region. When roused into action, the zygomatic major, which resides in the cheek, tugs the human lips upward and there it is—a silly grin, a beautiful beam, that wonderful smile (Jaffe, 2010). Those who witness this physical phenomenon respond by mirroring the action—they smile back. It's contagious and isn't that wonderful!

Research at the University of Missouri–Kansas City has shown that a smile does ten unique, if not amazing, things. Smiling makes a school leader: (1) look younger; (2) look thinner; (3) create a sense of well-being; (4) improve moods; (5) enhances relationships; (6) seem courteous, likable, trustworthy, and even competent; (7) increases one's life span; (8) avoid negative emotions; (9) feel better; and (10) positively influence others during difficult circumstances or situations (Selig, 2016; Ozono, Watabe, Yoshikawa, Nakashima, Rule, Ambady, & Adams, 2010).

Principals who start their daily work with one simple step, a smile, are much more apt to reflect a successful leader who has taken one of humanity's simplest expressions, though beautifully complex, and made the day a positive start for self and for others. Smiling establishes a positive mindset. Remember, "when you're smiling, the whole world smiles with you!" So, begin the day, the right way—SMILE!

DO THIS NEXT, EVERY DAY—MEET AND GREET!

Successful principals are actively and daily out and about—meeting and greeting members of the learning community, to include but not limited to students, faculty and staff, parents, community members, and business leaders. At all levels of schooling—elementary, middle, and high school—principals must begin their day with an important, if not critical, ritual or skill: meeting and greeting students as they arrive to start another day of learning. Students know which adults care, which have interest in them, and which principals are genuine in relating to their charges.

The very best principals work diligently each day to ensure they are seen and are engaged in interacting with students (the same is true of interactions with faculty and staff, parents, and community members). Walk into any school building anywhere across the nation and students will reveal in a heartbeat if they know their principal and if their principal knows them.

We spend a significant amount of time in schools visiting principal interns. It is a sad reflection upon a school principal when not one student offers a warm and welcoming "hello." Reason? The students have no idea that the individual passing them happens to be their principal! The principal is as much a stranger, to the students, as the accompanying visitor.

Such interactions pose a simple, yet straight-forward question: Why? Why are certain principals not known by their students? Answer: These principals are not people-centered—they fail to possess the essential people skills that serve as key effective leader elements. In fact, many of these school leaders often mistake office administrative duties as the sole work of the principal. So, what's a principal to do? First, recognize the deficiency. Second, learn how to gain the necessary people skills!

THE PEOPLE-CENTERED PRINCIPAL

If a principal is not a people person, or people-centered, is there hope? Good question! The answer resides within the individual. All skills can be gained if the individual who lacks the requisite measures is attuned to making essential adjustments in personality and habits. Changing personality traits is difficult, but most psychologists will agree, it's not an impossibility. Changing personality traits frequently correlates with the development of certain traits or habits (Vitelli, 2015). Thus, changing habits or traits to develop people skills is definitely doable—again, if the doer wishes (Roberts, 2016). That said, what are daily people skills that all principals must possess or work to acquire?

McQuerrey (2019) relates that good people skills are frequently defined as being: (1) an active listener; (2) able to communicate and/or relate to others on a personal and professional basis; (3) able to readily solve problems and make effective and appropriate decisions; (4) empathetic toward others; and (5) willing to collaboratively work with others toward a common goal, vision, and/or mission. Specifically, in almost every job or position, people skills have as much an impact on an individual's success as any technical skill (MindTools, 2019; Sorenson & Goldsmith, 2018; Pasqualis, 2017). What follows is an examination of the essential people skills necessary for a principal to succeed.

PEOPLE SKILLS: AN ESSENTIAL LEADERSHIP ELEMENT—WHAT PRINCIPALS MUST DO DAILY TO LEAD AND SUCCEED

First, a well-known fact: People skills are critical to a principal being successful. It's part of the daily job! People leaders extend interpersonal communication skills—knowing what to say, how to say it, when to say it, and who needs to be persuaded or motivated or simply informed. Possessing strong interpersonal communication skills is important to building and influencing relationships. Interpersonal communication skills are an essential daily element of any successful principalship.

People-centered leaders incorporate interpersonal communication skills by being able to listen, hear, and understand more actively and faster when an individual is attempting to explain a situation, concern, or circumstance. The people-centered principal does not become bored or exhibit wandering thoughts during the course of listening to another's conversation. The people-centered principal responds in a manner that ensures the leader has understood the feelings and intent of the other speaker.

People-centered leaders are able to decode barriers when interacting with others. In other words, principals who possess strong interpersonal communication skills fully grasp and/or translate what could very well end up becoming misperceptions, misinterpretations, or flatly ignored information. Such is exemplified in the following vignette.

* * *

BET THEY GOT A KICK OUT OF THAT! A BRIEF LEADERSHIP MODEL FOR EFFECTIVELY INCORPORATING INTERPERSONAL COMMUNICATION SKILLS

During a faculty meeting regarding a newly district-mandated, change-oriented instructional initiative, in which the principal and administrative team had spent prior hours in preparation for sharing with faculty and staff, Nora McPhee—one of the many teachers present—got up from her seat and wandered over to the soft-drink machine. After inserting her money in hopes of getting a quick shot of caffeine to use as a coping mechanism, a soft-drink can failed to emerge. Nora cursed under her breath and swiftly kicked the soft-drink machine. Max Dugan, her principal, stopped the presentation and asked: "Nora, are you alright?" Nora turned to her principal and sarcastically said: "Oh, sure! Bet they got a kick out of that!" and then walked out of the room.

Principal Dugan—who possesses strong people-centered, interpersonal communicative skills—should:

A. Offer to reimburse Nora for the change she lost.
B. Recognize Nora's nonverbal communication as revealed by kicking the soft-drink machine and extend to her an opportunity to speak privately about her "real" issue (the change-oriented, district-mandated instructional initiative).
C. Publicly discipline Nora for kicking the soft-drink machine, insisting that she apologize to the entire faculty and staff.
D. Recognize Nora's nonverbal communication as revealed in kicking the soft-drink machine and extend to her, lowering expectations, an opportunity to forgo the district-mandated instructional initiative/change.

The correct answer, from an interpersonal communication skills perspective is of course, (B). The principal, a people-centered leader, should immediately recognize Nora's nonverbal communication relates to her fear of the change process being initiated by the school district. Principal Max Dugan would be wise to interact with Nora and "dig deeper" as a means of determining the real, personal reason for her frustration and then help her work through the district-mandated instructional changes. And give her a refund!

* * *

People-centered leaders are effective in *respecting and managing differences* between members of the learning community. These principals possess this particular interpersonal skill which enables them to enjoy differences and make them work to the advantage of not only the school leader but also for everyone on campus. Key to this skill is the recognition that not all conflict is bad. Research has long proved that conflict can actually create significant and positive change (Hughes, Ginnett, & Curphy, 2019; Northouse, 2017; Marzano, Waters, & McNulty, 2010; Sorenson & Goldsmith, 2009; Heller, 1998).

People-centered leaders are often able to *properly and effectively manage conflict*. This can lead to creative, if not novel, problem-solving and decision-making processes, and can actually build stronger teams who are able to face and embrace personal and professional differences. Principal people leaders also incorporate essential interpersonal skills to *better understand people needs and points of view*. In doing so, a principal can often find solutions and bring about an "all-party" agreement in a positive, collaborative, and team-oriented manner.

People-centered leaders *exude a personal integrity*—an imperative interpersonal skill. Integrity is the bedrock of people-centered skills. Integrity is associated with leader honesty, truthfulness, honor, reliability, decency, trustworthiness, and being a morally decent human being. Basic interpersonal integrity can be summed up with the following leader-focused statements:

- *She frequently acknowledges us by saying "thank you" for the work we do!*
- *He always gives credit where credit is due. He is never one to step on the back of others by taking credit for something someone else has done!*
- *She recognizes the principalship is a position, not a title. She always puts the students and faculty first!*
- *He publicly and privately recognizes our contributions. He never fails to acknowledge our efforts.*
- *She genuinely creates a positive, harmonious, student-centered, and team-focused climate and culture!*

Finally, identified below are five additional people skills essential for a principal to daily lead and succeed:

1. *Be socially assertive and sustain confidence.* This aspect of interpersonal skills means overcoming any social anxiety, shyness, awkwardness, or

nervous tendencies. Being socially assertive and sustaining confidence means excelling in large or small group settings, showing a genuine interest in others, building rapport, and recognizing body language. The socially assertive or confident principal is positive, convincing, poised, self-assured, focused, and acts with clarity and insightfulness.
2. *Relate memorably to others.* Principals with strong interpersonal skills leave a positive lasting impression. They build rapport with others, create new friendships, remember names, reveal a keen sense of humor, and respect the positions of others, recognizing when it is important to agree to disagree.
3. *Exude strong communication skills.* As previously examined, this interpersonal skill is fundamental in a principal being able to speak publicly, persuade others, share a vision and/or idea, articulate a position, challenge ambiguity, and provide accurate and literal sense and meaning to situations.
4. *Be perceptive.* Highly interpersonal principals are good at reading people—decoding their emotional messages. These principals are masterful in daily recognizing how others feel and think. Highly perceptive principals are intuitive, empathetic, possess a high social and emotional intelligence, can effectively read body language and facial expressions, more readily understand the intentions of others, and are intuitive. In other words, these principals seldom miss social clues.
5. *Radiate charisma (charm) and influence.* These interpersonal principals are viewed as warm in personality, never mean-spirited or intimidating, and are recognized as being steadfast, thoughtful, reflective, and sincere. People principals are never apathetic, ambivalent, or aimless. Daily these school leaders are determined, achievement-oriented, motivated, and productive. They influence others to follow accordingly.

Principals who daily incorporate and utilize effective interpersonal communication "people" skills are much more apt to exhibit an essential leadership element which provides for clarity and understanding when it comes to interacting with others. These school principals frequently are confident, charming, influential, and perceptive. They are true leaders who can successfully engage, meet and greet, and use good humor for the betterment of the school community.

THE GOOD HUMOR MAN (WOMAN) SELLS MORE THAN ICE CREAM!

Many readers of this text may have no idea as to who or what was the Good Humor Man and Woman. Could we be referring to any number of comedy legends from the late Robin Williams, to Jerry Seinfeld, or even Steve Carell of *The Office* fame? How about Dave Chappelle, George Lopez, Sarah Silverman, or Jim Gaffigan? Maybe Tiffany Haddish, Kevin Hart, Chris Rock, or Michelle Wolf? Readers of this text certainly have their very own favorite comedian whose good humor has long kept people laughing!

However, the Good Humor Man and Woman referred to here was once a neighborhood staple—taking to the streets in a white ice cream truck, ringing a bell, and tempting, with a tasty frozen treat, kids of all ages! Yes, the Good Humor Man and Woman was on the block bringing a smile to the faces of those who could run fast enough to catch up with the traveling truck full of cold and delicious ice cream!

Must today's principal be a comedian to succeed as a school leader? Should today's principal be a confectioner selling good humor? Well, yes to some extent, on both accounts! Certainly, today's principal must possess the essential daily skill of being a salesperson for good humor. Good humor, in fact, should always be a part of any principal's leadership toolkit. Mark Twain wrote, "humor is mankind's greatest blessing" (BrainyQuote, 2001–2019b). Twain would certainly serve as an expert of good humor. Charlie Chaplin, silent-era comedic movie star, once stated: "A day without laughter is a day wasted" (BrainyQuote, 2001–2019c). Grenville Kleiser, as noted in the opening quote, was right: "Good humor . . . is a professional asset."

Good, positive humor permits a principal to better handle certain issues and school personnel in a nonthreatening manner. Good humor can very well be an effective leadership tool in diffusing moments that are stressful, negatively intensified, and potentially volatile. Good humor may serve as a means of permitting personnel, as well as principals, engaged in a difficult circumstance to laugh, or certainly to smile at themselves or the situation (Sorenson & Goldsmith, 2009). Additionally, principals must recognize that the research literature is explicit in recognizing the strong correlation between effective leadership and good, positive humor.

Dwight Eisenhower, a commanding military leader and the 34th president of the United States, correctly stated in the opening quote of this chapter: "A sense of humor is part of the art of leadership." Identified below are three examples as to why workplace humor is essential to school leadership.

1. *Leaders with a sense of humor often appear more competent.* Research conducted at the Bell Leadership Institute (2012) reveals that leaders who daily incorporate good, positive humor are often viewed as exhibiting a strong work ethic, are perceived as being better at managing circumstances or situations that could escalate out of control, and most interestingly, are viewed as taking charge.

Good humor is disarming, it builds stronger organizations, unleashes more creativity, and solves more problems. School personnel and principals that incorporate humor become more resilient, become more trustworthy of one another, and better develop a social bonding (Fazio, 2018; The Harvard Mahoney Neuroscience Institute, 2010).

Good humor and principal competency are more apt to be intertwined, leaving an impression with followers that unity can occur when there is teamwork, collaboration, and engagement resulting from good leader/follower humor (Campbell, 2018). A sense of humor is like a muscle—the more it's used, the stronger it becomes. After all, it has long been said that "laughter is the best medicine!"

2. *Laughter brings people together.* Recall the old saying: "We know funny when we see it or hear it!" True statement. Doesn't everyone know funny? Granted, people have different tastes when it comes to comedy. What makes one person laugh may make another person cringe. So, if school principals understand that possessing a sense of humor makes for sound leadership, how does one appropriately and tastefully bring humor to the school site-level?

First and foremost, principals must know the individual(s) involved well enough to predict a reaction, because the infusion of humor could negatively affect a person if the humor is perceived as being distasteful, off-color, or demeaning. Humor must never be at the expense of others. If a principal needs a tutorial in what is or is not a distasteful joke, an off-color story, or a demeaning witticism, that principal doesn't need or deserve to be in a leadership role!

Additionally, humor can never be incorporated by school leaders as a form of disguised aggression as such creates resentment, if not increased anger. Inappropriate humor will reduce followers' perceptions of leader competence. Successful principals incorporate uplifting or good humor and always recognize the following: if principals find it funny to laugh at someone's foibles and shortcomings, it is best to make that someone themselves. Be reminded of what is occasionally found inside a Chinese fortune cookie: "He who learns to laugh at himself never ceases to be amused!"

Here's what is known about humor: It's good for people to laugh! School principals and personnel who laugh daily are healthier. They are more productive. They miss work less often. Good humor relaxes the body, provides objectivity, increases learning, and is relaxing (Mayo Clinic, 2016). Humor, as already shared, has been linked with effective leadership. Daily laughter improves a school's climate, making life at work much more positive.

Humor, if not laughter, helps principals and school personnel seek goal clarity, improve problem-solving, and reduce conflict as well as stress (Rise, 2018). Life's already too short, so laugh a little—shoot, laugh a lot! Impress a colleague or a group of colleagues by telling a good joke! Here's a silly one about two educators—a married couple: Peg, a school principal, and Chester, a teacher. The couple meets with a therapist who says: "So, tell me, what brings you two here, today?

CHESTER: My truck!
PEG: See, it's really difficult living with him. He's so literal!

Okay, go ahead and roll the eyes, but there was a slight smile, wasn't there? And remember, laughter *is* the best medicine! A smile happens to be the second-best medicine!

3. *Humor reveals a human side.* Principals would be wise to let down their guard from time-to-time. People love leaders who joke (Buchanan, 2018). So, give humor a stage. Begin faculty meetings with an occasional joke or a funny story as related to the group, or to self, or what is about to be a topic of discussion. Be receptive to holding meetings or faculty gatherings at locales that foster fun. Principals who confess a personal weakness and tell a funny story about themselves in the spirit of vulnerability and transparency reveal a human side. Always remember and never forget—be a school principal who knows when to use good humor and when not to!

Three concluding notes. First, a warning. Second, further research implications regarding leader humor. Third, a warm-hearted, concluding laugh!

1. Principals must know when and where to incorporate humor. Good humor is positive and uplifting, at times appropriate when diffusing certain situations. Humor that is in bad taste or disrespectful is not good, nor funny. Again, it's demeaning. Additionally, a principal who is viewed as always cracking jokes may not be taken seriously. Attempting to defuse all situations with humor means the principal is not accurately reading or responding to certain conditions or circumstances.

   Good, warm-hearted humor can be effective. Silly, malicious, and/or demeaning humor is not representative of any appropriate or effective leadership skill. Successful principals regularly utilize good humor but always in a tasteful, professional manner.

2. As previously indicated, good, respectful humor can serve as one of a principal's best survival tools! Good, warm-hearted, and appropriate humor, as a leadership tool and technique, works and has long been positively confirmed in the research literature (Avolio, Howell, & Sosik, 1999; Hughes, Ginnett, & Curphy, 2019; Robbins & Judge, 2017; Romero & Cruthirds, 2006; and Sala, 2003). Good humor is actually quite serious and has been determined to be one of the ten habits of highly effective leaders, relating to organizational contentment and deeper levels of emotional joy and intellectual engagement within and across an organization (Caulfield, Kidd, & Kocher, 2000; and Gibson, 2003).

3. Now, a concluding chuckle: Did you hear the one about the man who telephoned the doctor and said, "Quick, my pregnant wife's going into labor! What should I do?" The doctor said, "Is this her first child?" The man responded, "Well, no. This is her husband!"

FINAL THOUGHTS

Successful principals do this first each day—they smile! Smiling makes a school leader look younger, thinner, creates a sense of well-being, improves moods, enhances relationships, positively influences others, and increases life spans. Next, successful principals daily meet and greet members of the learning community. Additionally, these principals work diligently each day to be seen and to interact with students, faculty and staff, parents, and community members.

Successful principals are people-centered. Effective people skills are defined as being an active listener, effectively communicating with and/or relating to others, solving problems and making decisions, showing empathy, and collaboratively working with others toward a common goal, vision, and/or mission.

Successful principals possess people skills that are essential to effective daily leadership and overall professional success. People skills include being persuasive, motivated, and decoding barriers that could lead to misperceptions or misinterpretations. As people leaders, successful principals respect and manage differences between members of the learning community, properly and effectively manage conflict, understand people's needs and points of views, and exude a personal integrity. Successful principals are also socially assertive and confident, relate memorably to others, and are charming and engaging.

Successful principals who engage in good, positive humor, are more apt to handle certain school personnel issues in a nonthreatening manner. They can very well diffuse moments that are stressful, negatively intensified, and/or potentially volatile. School leaders who exhibit a positive sense of humor often appear more competent, bring people together, reveal a human side, and are frequently very successful.

DISCUSSION QUESTIONS

1. What does the research literature reveal to principals and prospective principals regarding smiling as well as daily meeting and greeting members of the learning community? Provide specificity in responding to the question.

2. McQuerrey (2019) postulates that good people skills are essential to principal leadership success. Notably, five people skills define an effective people-centered leader. Of the five skills, as noted on pages 93–94, which one might be considered most essential to principal and team success? Explain. Which of the defined people skills might be personally targeted for professional growth and development?
3. In the chapter section entitled "People Skills: An Essential Leadership Element—What Principals Must Do Daily to Lead and Succeed," five critical leadership elements are defined and detailed. Examine the five elements and place in priority order. Then, defend the newly created priority listing.
4. Why is it important, as a people-centered individual, in a school leadership role, to be confident, socially assertive, perceptive, and memorable to others? Explain.
5. Examine the three professional attributes (see pages 95–97), as related to possessing a sense of humor. Explain how these three attributes daily enhance the school leadership role. In other words, how do these attributes and corresponding descriptors aid a principal in being a successful leader? Be specific in answering the question.
6. Now, think of a good, wholesome, and humorous joke. Share it with your colleagues! Did the joke bring on a smile, a wide grin, or a belly-laugh? Does everyone feel better? Remember, life is short. Laugh often and smile frequently—while you still have your teeth!

CASE STUDY APPLICATION—
TEST YOUR PEOPLE SKILLS

This case study application is different from those previously presented. It is actually an opportunity to test those people-skills that make a school principal a more successful, if not exceptional, leader. Take the brief 15-statement test to better assess current skill levels.

Directions

Examine each of the statements below and enter a score which best describes you as a people-skill leader. Respond to each statement accurately—how you, as a school leader, are in actuality people-centered, and not how you believe you should be. Scoring interpretations will follow the statements presented.

Listed below are the scoring categories with numerical rankings. Place the identified numerical ranking in the blank prior to each statement based on "real" people-centered perceptions of yourself.

1 (Very Often)   2 (Often)   3 (Sometimes)   4 (Seldom)   5 (Never)

As a principal or prospective principal:

_____ I am certain that members of the learning community know about my contributions toward a positive, students-first harmonious climate and open culture.

_____ I display the same standards of behavior that I expect from others.

_____ I examine the needs of the members of the learning community, decide what is to be said, and determine the best method of saying it.

_____ I follow the decisions of the instructional team rather than inject my own ideas or opinions.

_____ I consider how members of the learning community perceive a problem or issue.

_____ I collaborate with all members of the learning community when solving problems and making decisions.

_____ I often say "thank you" to members of the learning community, giving credit where credit is due.

_____ I pay attention to the body language of members of the learning community.

_____ I speak first and then think afterwards.

_____ I consider, during conflicts, how to preserve relationships but get my needs met.

_____ I actively listen and provide feedback, often asking members of the learning community to provide further explanation so I can better understand issues.

_____ I do what is essential to ensure that I get ahead as a school leader.

_____ I, working collaboratively with members of the learning community, determine the best solution to a problem in an effort to make the very best decision.

_____ I often create more problems when attempting to resolve a personnel conflict.

_____ I provide feedback to members of the learning community that is an accurate and helpful reflection of what has been either observed or learned.

Scoring Interpretations

15–35

Your people skills, as a school leader or potential school leader, are inhibiting your ability to develop strong interpersonal relationships with members of the learning community. This is also impeding your ability to develop a more collaborative and facilitative approach to achieving team-centered and organization-oriented goals. The calculated score further indicates you are limiting your own professional growth and development as well as career advancement.

36–55

Your people skills, as a school leader, are enabling you to work well with members of the learning community. Your collaborative and facilitative approaches to leading indicate personal and professional growth. However, you may still be ensuring your personal and professional needs are met first. Also, when you are stressed and/or pressured to solve problems and make decisions, you instinctively revert back to a more authoritative approach to leading. In other words, "I'll figure this out myself!" Both of these noted developmental considerations remain areas to target for continued growth.

56–75

Your people skills, as a school leader, are on-target! You recognize how essential collaboration and facilitation are when working with members of the school community. You understand and put to work the old adage: "All of us are smarter than any one of us!" Members of the learning community appreciate and respect you for this leadership approach to problem-solving and decision-making. Finally, recognize the importance of continuing to enhance your people skills. By doing so, you will become a more successful school leader and your team will be more motivated, inspired, and achievement-oriented.

Chapter 7

Daily Step #7
Build Capacity

"Teachers and administrators attribute much of their success to the leadership opportunities that occur through collaborative work."
—Jonathan Eckert (*Leading Together*, 2018, p. 78)

"Building capacity can have a profound effect, making life-changing differences for principals, teachers, and students." —Pete Hall and Alisa Simeral, 2008, p. 114

BUILDING CAPACITY IN EDUCATION

"I'm hoping we can collaborate and work together," a new principal stated. The new principal then said: "We must build capacity." Two key statements by a principal with the best of intentions. The statements serve as a reminder to readers that thinking, stating, and doing are three separate factors key to a principal's overall ability to build capacity. Here's what is known: Building capacity is a daily step, but it isn't always easy.

There are numerous issues, influences, and circumstances which are likely to interfere when a principal is attempting to positively impact the capacity (the amount of competence, aptitude, and ability) of a learning community, specifically, when it comes to teaching, leading, and learning. Jonathan Eckert, in the opening quote, was right: Administrators and teachers successfully build capacity at the campus level when working collaboratively and leading a team-oriented effort to positively and effectively benefit students. Hall and Simeral (2008) noted the necessity for building capacity at the campus level. The effects on leading, teaching, and learning can be substantial. Moreover, capacity-building, through reflective practice, translates into real student achievement gains (Hall & Simeral, 2017). All begs the question: What, exactly, is capacity-building?

Capacity Defined

The term "building capacity" is frequently incorporated throughout educational circles, within the research literature, and certainly espoused in most school settings. The term is often used in reference to perceived abilities, skills, and the expertise of school-site leaders, teachers, and staff members. Most commonly, the term relates to an individual's or team's ability to execute or accomplish a specific deed or process—such as leading a school-improvement effort, or teaching more effectively, or perfecting the instructional program, or ensuring student achievement is successfully progressing. The term, "building capacity," can also encompass a quality of adaptation—the ability of a school principal and/or teacher(s) to regularly and effectively develop, progress, and/or improve.

Simply defined, "building capacity" refers to any instructionally-oriented effort established to improve the abilities, skills, and expertise of educators. To best understand the meaning of "capacity," it is imperative to further define the word with related terms: capability, aptitude, level of competence, proficiency, skill, fitness, expertise, experience, means, and/or potential. Principals must never call upon others (administrative team, academic coaches, faculty, or staff) to "build capacity" without describing precisely what capacities should be improved, or in what area (instruction or curriculum, for example) the improvement must occur.

Car Analogy #1

Possibly, the following analogy will bring our thoughts closer together relative to the subject of the meaning of capacity and the taking of daily steps to build capacity. A principal says to himself: "I'm thinking tonight that I'll tell my spouse I believe there will be a brand-new SUV sitting in our driveway by morning." Possible? Surely so, if he goes out tonight and buys one! Probable? On an educator's salary with an increasingly tight budget? Not likely! Possibly the brand-new SUV in the driveway the next morning can become a reality if the marital team—working together—first develop a plan, initiate a process, save their money, and budget accordingly by investing wisely in a highly recognized, positively consumer-rated, reasonably priced, and road-tested model. Such is an example, if not a means, of building capacity.

Let's return to the principal statements about building capacity in the opening paragraph. Conceivably, the new principal should verbalize: "I think we can, if we work together as a team. I'm willing to say we can, if we collaborate. I do believe we can, if I facilitate a daily process through a series of successful team-oriented and capacity-building efforts."

Bottom line: Building capacity is NEVER impossible! That said, if a principal intends to build capacity within and across the learning community, she/he must recognize and understand why and how the capacity-building process is an essential every-day step to developing and maintaining a successful teaching, leading, and learning environment. To begin to better comprehend the process, let's describe "capacity"—from a "how and by what means" perspective.

SUCCESSFUL PRINCIPALS BUILD CAPACITY FOR EVERYONE'S ACHIEVEMENT, EVERY DAY

Research has long proven that coupled together, principal leadership and teacher effectiveness serve as the number one determinant of successful student academic achievement (Bambrick-Santoyo, 2018; Desravines, Aquino, & Fenton, 2016; .Eckert, 2018; Guthrie & Schuermann, 2010; Hoy & Hoy, 2012; Marzano, Waters, & McNulty, 2010; Shaw, 2012; Sorenson & Goldsmith, 2018; Sorenson, Goldsmith, Méndez, & Maxwell, 2011).

For principals to meet their goal of student success, they must daily lead, guide, direct, and support the growth and development of teachers as well as the instructional program. The question remains: how, and by what means, must a principal successfully lead, manage, and support real, tangible, and practical professional development, especially during an era of fiscal constraint, conservative funding, political wrangling, ever-changing standards, constant student testing, school accountability practices, disputed contracts and associated strikes, and chaotic prescriptive directives which all too often serve to stifle the most creative teaching techniques, strategies, and instructional methodologies?

The answer: Build, on a daily basis, a capacity for the success for all members of the learning community. Again, how and by what means?

The How, and By What Means?

Building capacity within and across the learning community involves a principal developing intentional relationships through reflective processes, skill development, instructional modeling, and intensive feedback. Hall (2014) identifies four stages by which teaching, leading, and learning capacity is increased: 1) Recognize educators are frequently *unaware* of their deficiencies, their need for professional growth and skill development; 2) Become *conscious* of certain professional areas (weaknesses) that must be targeted for growth; 3) Take *action* to bring about improvement (do what must be done to advance, expand, and/or increase skill abilities); and 4) Enhance and ensure personal and professional *refinement*—in other words, make modifications to the ways in which educators mature professionally, ways in which a fine-tuning or tweaking of professional abilities can occur.

Car Analogy #2

To better understand, think in terms of your car. Initially, you're driving along and all seems well. The engine is quiet, almost silent, as you scurry across town. You are completely *unaware* that a problem is developing. You don't recognize the issue, you're not *conscious* that something is wrong. You don't sense it. But there is a problem. Then, you feel and hear something. The car doesn't seem to handle correctly or even sound right. It's a grinding sound, or a thumping or whistling noise, or a ratty-tat-tat vibration that's anything but normal. You suddenly recognize that *action* must be taken.

Next, while not necessarily certain as to what's the problem, you decide to drive the car to a nearby repair shop. The mechanic listens to the engine and immediately recognizes that the timing belt is slipping, and thus the mechanic makes the necessary *refinement*—he repairs or replaces what is broken. Sometimes, our work (and the work of others) is broken. Our work, their work, needs refinement, needs to be adjusted or fine-tuned, so we can operate better! Humans, like cars, can very well operate in a superior manner when proper adjustments (research-based, student-centered best practices) are made. Like cars, our capacity to improve is greatly enhanced when a problem is identified, addressed, and then corrected.

* * *

A FINE-TUNING IS REQUIRED: A BRIEF LEADERSHIP MODEL FOR BUILDING TEACHER CAPACITY

Les Nessman, a slight, balding, bespectacled journalism teacher at Arthur Carlson High School, always wears a bow tie—maintaining a dignified professional appearance. While professional in his attire, Mr. Nessman is anything but in his professional duties as a teacher. He is more apt to be incompetent, often posing as an obstacle to student success. Yet, he seldom recognizes his ineptitude.

Mr. Nessman makes glaring errors, overlooks important school news stories that should be included within the *Cat Paw* campus newspaper, often having his students focus on outside of school activities that are less than meaningful or newsworthy—such as having students produce a news story about a friend's pig that can use one of his front hooves to do addition and subtraction.

Mr. Nessman longs to move up into a school administrative position. Numerous years ago, he earned his master's degree and principal certificate. He even proudly announces to differing teachers that he, like the school's principal, has his own private office. Such is true, but most journalism teachers do have their own private office within the journalism classroom, often in simulation of an editor's desk/office in a "real" newsroom.

The principal of Arthur Carlson High School, Dr. Bailey Quarters, is working with Mr. Nessman in an attempt to build the instructional capacity of the teacher. Listed below are some of the capacity-building, fine-tuning processes being implemented by Principal Quarters.

____ Spending more time observing the instructional process in the journalism classroom.

____ Conducting formal and informal observations (walk-throughs) of Mr. Nessman.

____ Providing timely, meaningful feedback, based on the teacher observations.

____ Affording opportunities for Mr. Nessman to be reflective about his teaching methods, techniques, and strategies.

____ Leading face-to-face conversations whereby teacher and principal can reflect and consider instructional approaches.

____ Developing a model approach to teaching whereby "master" teachers and academic coaches, along with the principal herself, present lessons to aid Mr. Nessman in becoming more adept and effective as a practitioner.

____ Helping Mr. Nessman recognize the need to be open to continuous learning.

____ Monitoring how Mr. Nessman plans, scrutinizes, and reflects upon his teaching actions and learning tasks. Helping Mr. Nessman become more aware of how his thoughts, strategies, feelings, and actions affect others—notably, his students.

____ Aiding Mr. Nessman in clarifying teaching and student issues, solving instructional and learning problems, striving for accuracy in teaching and learning, and ascertaining how to question and pose instructionally-focused and field-of-practice journalism scenarios to the students.

____ Communicating effectively with Mr. Nessman by actively listening with understanding and empathy, yet never negating the highest of expectations.

____ Encouraging, if not directing, Mr. Nessman to take responsible instructional risks—attempting new, different, and creative approaches to teaching and learning.

___ Working with Mr. Nessman to develop an attitude of persistence and perseverance. In other words, seeing teaching tasks, methods, techniques, and strategies through to completion—always seeking research-based, student-centered methods and best practices to reach the goal of being a highly competent teacher.

* * *

The Top 11 Capacity-Building Tools

Sorenson, Goldsmith, and DeMatthews (2016) in their text, *The Principal's Guide to Time Management: Instructional Leadership in the Digital Age*, underscore the need for effective leadership relative to building teacher capacity by noting first and foremost the fostering of democratic ideals across the school and in the classroom as a means of modeling behavior that is nourishing by building up the capacities of all members of the learning community.

Hadden (2019) reiterates a long-known fact: principals lead the way they were led. Teachers teach the way they were taught. Therefore, intuitively, teachers lead in their classrooms the way they are led by their principals. Principals must build capacity in their faculty and staff by utilizing strategies that are designed to invite participation, embrace diversity, and focus on specific leadership tactics and approaches as examples of how to create a culture of not only building capacity, but one of expanding capacity.

Listed below are 11 capacity-building tools that serve to daily strengthen and better develop instruction, improve teaching, enhance leading, and increase student achievement through multiple measures of evaluation.

Tool #1—Incorporate reflective conversations and instructional coaching. Reflection and coaching serve as means of moving teachers forward in their professional work to better ensure student academic success and achievement.

Tool #2—Develop specifically defined rubrics for formal and informal observations. Such rubrics better inspire teachers to look deeper into their practice and to discover areas that need to be targeted for professional growth and development. Many school systems incorporate state developed/mandated appraisal and observation forms with defined rubrics.

Tool #3—Align teacher evaluation/appraisal results to inform professional development opportunities. Examples exist, to include but not limited to the following: (1) listening to an instructionally-oriented presentation by a "master" teacher colleague and/or an educational specialist; (2) planning instruction after analyzing student data; (3) reading or participating in a book study (examples: *Visible Learning for Teachers* by John Hattie;

Teach Like a Champion by Doug Lemov; *Leverage Leadership 2.0* by Paul Bambrick-Santoyo; or *Breakthrough Principals* by Jean Desravines, Jaime Aquino, and Benjamin Fenton); (4) Engaging in a webcast; (5) interacting with and receiving support from an academic coach; or (6) participating in a peer classroom walkthrough process, observing "master" teachers and collecting evidence to support the implementation of best-practice instructional methods and techniques.

Tool #4—Incorporate tech-tools to be better informed of student progress. Teachers can be trained to utilize district-made spread sheets or commercially developed software to track student work and recognize when a group of students are performing poorly in a particular objective, thus highlighting what teachers must focus on in their own instruction. Such tools serve to improve not only student performance, but teacher performance.

Software such as Google Docs assists with collegial conversations, providing for constant feedback between teachers and administrators, allowing teachers to regularly adjust instructional coursework and learning sequences.

Other tech tools include utilization of e-Tablets and cell phones, as well as software such as Excel, DocsServer Document Management, etc. Numerous websites offer suggestions, recommendations, and ideas for both principals and teachers. Here's one: www.redbytes.in/best-apps-for-teachers-and-educators/. Principals and teachers have many viable tech choices—just find the right website, along with hardware and software tools, to meet the needs of all parties.

Tool #5—Ensure conversations will affirm instructional work. While educators work more and more in a world of prescriptive and oftentimes isolated teaching, principals must recognize there is an "art of teaching"—elements of instruction that aren't always measured by an evaluation instrument. To best build teaching and learning capacity, principals must always provide opportunities for teachers to *talk* in depth about the chosen logic used in making instructional decisions—why a teacher decides to choose a certain method or strategy or technique or technology to convey new learning. These conversations must be held, pre- and post-evaluation conference.

Tool #6—Develop solid relationships with faculty, staff, parents, students, and community members. Building capacity within and across a community of learners begins with the development of important, if not essential, relationships.

To effectively develop such relationships, a principal must (1) establish clear expectations; (2) listen carefully and actively to all members of the learning community; (3) set a positive, ethical, and moral example as the campus lead learner; (4) develop high levels of trust; (5) collaborate and facilitate; (6) focus on students, first and foremost; (7) give respect to gain respect; (8) maintain a "people-person" demeanor; (9) trust but verify and inspect what is expected; and (10) showcase the effective instructional processes being accomplished by faculty—always giving credit, never taking undue credit!

Tool #7—Ensure campus committees have meaningful work that benefits the entire learning community. Committee parameters must always be established before any work of the committee convenes. Committee parameters should include factors associated with (1) start and end times; (2) funding as is necessary; (3) defined authority and responsibility; (4) required committee member roles and skills; and (5) reporting periods and deadlines.

Tool #8—Accept suggestions and criticism and be open to change. Give up the lead and be more collaborative. Compromise is a means of efficiency and success. Shared leadership equates to responsibility in decision-making and problem-solving. Such builds the capacity of the learning community. Additionally, diverging opinions must be heard and given proper consideration. Remember, authoritarian rule is demoralizing, if not defeating.

Tool #9—Delegate authority and encourage autonomy as a means of distributing power and influence. However, recall again, successful principals delegate, but they also "trust but verify" and "they inspect what they expect!" Also recall that old adage: "All of us are smarter than any one of us!" Delegating is much more than a downloading of tasks on someone else—that's called "dumping."

Effective and appropriate delegation provides not only authority to complete a task or series of tasks, it also provides essential resources, problem-solving and decision-making authority, and a level of accountability. Most important, delegation provides opportunities for others to develop leadership capabilities and contribute to the capacity-building efforts of a principal and team.

Tool #10—Mentor! Mentor! Mentor! Successful principals believe in building capacity by what Fullan (2003) equates to as a steadiness in leadership. In other words, keep the boat afloat but always steaming ahead—moving, working, and engaging with an ever-reliable focus, tendency, and objective. Here, mentoring cannot be overemphasized. The development and creation of talent and experience will always be a crucial factor for improving teaching, leading, and learning.

However, principals who properly mentor others, resulting in the development of remarkable proteges, find greater assurance in the realization that the sustainability of collaboratively developed initiatives will better ensure increased student achievement and an improved teaching, leading, and learning community.

Tool #11—Take time for reflection, meditation, and even prayer. Principals live and work at a fast pace. Their time is precious, their tasks are numerous, and their daily demands are unrelenting. There are never enough hours in the day and all too often, principals realize there may not be enough time to accomplish, even in the span of a career or lifetime, all that must be done. The business of schooling, principal productivity, time-management, meetings and deadlines, and keeping all the plates spinning in mid-air frequently describe, if not define, the principalship.

As a result, health is often neglected; some marriages suffer, if not fail; a principal's own children and family members lack attention; and spiritual life goes by the wayside. Truth be told, principals recognize these circumstances and are concerned. In fact, chances are, principals promise they will make essential changes in life, ensure more meaningful interactions and attentions, and restore a critical balance between work, family, and play.

These promises are, regretfully, often unfulfilled. Life and career go forward. Trouble looms. Consequences? A heart attack, cancer, marital breakdown, unexpected changes in supervisory leadership, or undesired transfer readily bring about a time of contemplation. Better late than never, right? However, does it have to be this way? Is this what life as a school principal is all about? Must such be an expected outcome? All questions which require answers.

Consider the following: How better for a principal to recognize early in career or for that matter, anytime during career, the value of reflection (see chapter 8), meditation, serious consideration, and even prayer. Successful principals understand the importance of time spent thinking, ruminating, and engaging in serious reflection. Successful principals seek quiet time to contemplate the cards life has dealt them.

Successful principals daily engage in reflective thinking. No doubt, they too, have many trials and tribulations competing for their attention, aspects of career requiring careful thought and wise decision-making. These successful school leaders take time to clear the mind, escape worldly distractions, and thus, concentrate attention away from busy career, the inevitable confusions of life, as well as the ultimate, if not sometimes bitter, disappointments of being a leader. So, what is the answer?

One successful leader prescribes the following: Each evening, take a walk out in the fields, meditating-reflecting-ruminating-thinking. This leader states: "Urgent and pressing school business will always demand attention, and face it, will get it! However, principals must take time, daily, to reflect and meditate, or pray about the issues of career and life. Doing so will arrest one's personal dilemmas and issues of heart. But remember, it's in the quiet of the evening (or early morning for that matter) that reflection and meditation on matters can better resolve life's current or future problems" (Goldsmith, 2019).

Taken to heart and incorporated at the school-site level, these Top 11 Capacity-Building Tools can better affirm principals are daily targeting, developing, and strengthening teaching, leading, and learning skills and processes. These multiple measures, along with the additional capacity-building techniques, methods, and strategies, as detailed throughout this chapter and previous chapters, will better ensure principals, leadership teams, and teachers are working together to increase student academic achievement.

CAPACITY-BUILDING AND SUSTAINABILITY

Building capacity, as previously examined, is a continuous process—sometimes it seems, even to the most successful principals, an unremitting struggle! Actually, capacity-building is all about sustainability—a principal having the ability, knowledge, skill, and expertise to endure, weather the conditions, and maintain the course. Identified below are several additional capacity-building strategies that will aid a principal and team in sustaining daily positive change by enhancing the capability, aptitude, proficiency, and competency—all for the best benefit of students!

Principals must focus on:

- Building a strong and enduring instructional foundation based on strategic research-based best practices;
- Integrating school constructs that have previously been isolated aspects of teaching, leading, and learning. These constructs include:
  - Monitoring and enhancing organizational climate and culture.
  - Incorporating data-driven instruction.
  - Providing constant and consistent teacher observations and essential feedback.
  - Developing and engaging in professional development that is based on data analyses and designed to provide teaching and learning interventions and instructional delivery support.
- Identifying problems, root causes of instructional impediments and/or failures;
- Solving the identified problems—demonstrating a sense of urgency, collecting relevant data, initiating research-based, student-centered programs and initiatives, and leveraging expertise from on- and off-campus specialists;
- Creating an environment where ongoing change is norm. Successful principals recognize that nothing can ever be "nonnegotiable"—NOTHING! Every aspect of an instructional program must be regularly assessed, evaluated, and changed as necessary, to best benefit student academic achievement. Such is a very difficult aspect of capacity-building. Why? Because multiple stakeholders will have to change ingrained behaviors. Remember, no one ever said being a principal would be easy;

- Engaging and enabling the learning community to recognize and be organized and prepared to:
  - Conceive a vision for creative instructional change and urgency.
  - Form a powerful coalition based upon the notion of "Yes we can and yes we will!" Principals must build strong instructional programs and guide teams to ensure better teaching and learning. Mr. or Ms. Principal—you must lead, guide, direct, and motivate!
  - Empower each other by adapting and adopting leadership roles and responsibilities.
  - Never let up or give up! Buy-in, active involvement, and never conceding must be organizational and personal mantras if students, faculty, instructional programs, and even principals are to succeed.

FINAL THOUGHTS

Successful principals build capacity by understanding the true meaning of the term, *capacity*. These principals recognize that building capacity at the school-site level is frequently related to a faculty and staff's abilities, skills, and expertise. Building capacity relates to any instructionally-oriented and directed effort to improve the capability, aptitude, level of competence, proficiency, experience, and/or potential of a school's leading, teaching, and learning team.

Successful principals acknowledge that the daily effort of building capacity isn't easy but neither is it impossible. These principals are intent on building capacity for the success of all by helping others become aware of their deficiencies—their need for professional growth and skill development; by becoming more conscious of what exactly must be targeted for growth; by taking appropriate action to better ensure improvement; and by making professional refinements or modifications to best ensure increased student achievement.

Successful principals incorporate the Top 11 Capacity-Building Tools. These tools aid a principal each day, for example, with incorporating reflective listening and conversations, the utilization of teacher evaluations to inform professional development, the integration of tech-tools to ensure student progress and achievement, the cultivation of "people-person" relationships, and the mentoring of team members to develop the sustainability of instructional programs.

Finally, successful principals lead with veracity, tenacity, and perseverance. These principals daily lead in their efforts to not only build capacity at the campus level, they lead to ensure the success of all—students, teachers, parents—every member of the learning community!

DISCUSSION QUESTIONS

1. Re-read this chapter's opening quote from the book, *Leading Together* (2018) by Jonathan Eckert. Why is collaboration so important to the capacity-building capabilities of a school principal and team? Support your response.
2. Contemplate and then identify in writing a real-life scenario whereby it would be prudent for a principal to implement the four stages (*unaware*, *conscious*, *action*, and *refinement*) by which the teaching, leading, and learning capacity of a school can be increased. Next, apply the four stages to the real-life scenario identified. Then, indicate specifically how the four stages could result in actual capacity-building relative to teaching, leading, and learning. Remember to ponder, specifically, *what's a principal to do*?
3. Consider how, by what means, Principal Bailey Quarters—in the chapter scenario "A Fine Tuning Is Required: A Brief Leadership Model for Building Teacher Capacity"—could best afford opportunities for Mr. Nessman to be reflective about his teaching methods, techniques, and strategies. Explain in detail.
4. Reflect upon the chapter section entitled "The Top 11 Capacity-Building Tools," and specifically identify which of the tools would best serve a principal in working with Mr. Les Nessman, journalism teacher at Arthur Carlson High School, to improve his teaching, leading, and learning capacities. Be specific in answering.
5. Which five of the 12 capacity-building processes being implemented by Principal Bailey Quarters in the section "A Fine Tuning Is Required: A Brief Leadership Model for Building Teacher Capacity" are to be perceived as essential, if not critical, to a principal successfully ensuring an overall improvement in the capability, aptitude, level of competence, proficiency, experience, and/or potential of a school's leading, teaching, and learning team? Explain.

CASE STUDY APPLICATION—CANADIAN GEESE: AN EDUCATIONAL LEADERSHIP ALLEGORY

Late one cold and dreary Saturday afternoon, Paul Reven, principal at L. E. White School, sat behind his desk in the school office. Principal Reven had been on campus reviewing paperwork prior to the start of the next workweek. Looking up from his paperwork, the principal sipped on a warm cup of coffee and began to think about how he could build capacity, on a daily basis, at L. E. White School.

Mr. Reven decided to get up and stretch his legs, maybe put on his coat and step outside for a brisk, yet chilly, walk. He soon found himself walking across the empty campus parking lot—cold and alone. While making the hurried walk, the principal noticed flying across the grey, cloud-filled sky a flock of Canadian geese.

Mr. Reven smiled as he was reminded of an old allegory (a fable, tale, story) he had once heard during his days at Union State University where he had pursued his principal certification. The principal recalled how he had excelled in the leadership program at Union State and mused out loud: "Those were the days." Days that had been rigorous, yet interesting and enlightening, with each class session filled with the highest of learning expectations.

Again, the Canadian geese allegory filled his mind. But now he was beginning to shiver—thinking how cold he was and how cold it must be at the altitude of the flying geese. Mr. Reven wandered back toward the school building, came to his office door and walked inside to a most welcomed warmth. "That allegory," the principal thought again. He couldn't get it out of his mind.

Mr. Reven removed his coat, sat down at his desk, and reconsidered the tale one more time, running it over and over in his mind. What a parallel—the allegory and a desired correlation relative to him and the school's instructional team. The principal said to himself: "I think I'll write it down." Glancing at his laptop, the principal began to recount the allegory, hands now warmed up and ready to type. The more he recounted, the faster he typed, becoming absorbed with the visionary aspects of the old story. He wrote:

> The lead goose, tired of many trips south from the northern freezing winters of Canada, recognized it was time to share the lead role with others in a flock of determined geese. The leader thought: "My leadership capacity must be shared. I need to relinquish this lead role and permit the fellow members of this great flock to utilize their own stored up strength, knowledge, and capacity to keep us on a straight and narrow path, southward toward a warmer and more pleasant locale." That's when the lead goose relayed to the others: "My time is up. I've brought us far. We've made much progress but there are miles and miles to go before we reach our long-coveted destination. Who's up to the challenge of leading, today?"
>
> "I am" said one of the geese with a special talent of flying straight and maintaining a proper course, even when the going got rough. With that strong declaration, the lead goose responded in kind: "Great! I'm proud to learn that one of our very own has the specialized skills necessary to help lead us on our journey! Take over, my good friend."
>
> The lead goose then relinquished the leadership role, made a move back so the responsive and reliable next goose could swing into place—a place of leading the rest of the team. Little by little, all along the arduous journey, one goose after another accepted the leadership role. Ultimately, the flock of geese reached their desired destination but not without members of the team accepting the high expectation of sharing the leadership role and associated responsibility.

Principal Reven finished typing his story, leaned back in his chair, and thought: "I must be the lead goose that rotates back into the formation and permits another goose to fly forward and assume a leadership point of position. This is a lesson that must not be lost here at L. E. White School. I am charged with building capacity among our professionals as each individual on our team has special talents, interests, skills, and abilities. Certainly, there are a myriad of abilities which can help me build capacity here at school. What I need to develop is a culture of shared leadership. I have to be more receptive to giving up that old traditional notion of 'I'm the sole leader—I'm the only one to always take the lead and keep the lead.'"

Sometimes such an admission is difficult, especially for those with tenacious Type A personalities. Some school leaders may view democracy at the school-site level as a threat to their very own power and status. However, in reality, such is not the case. The skill of capacity building requires a service mentality—one in which a principal recognizes the need for collaboration and facilitation. A principal intent on building capacity within and across the professional ranks must possess an ability to let go and share the leadership responsibility (recall chapter 3). Doing so is most conducive to not only building capacity but to also shaping a positive and open culture where the potential for leadership in and from others is realized and expanded.

Application Questions

1. What specific leadership message does the allegory espouse?
2. How does the leadership message in the Canadian geese allegory compare with the notion of building capacity in schools?
3. Identify emerging issues that correlate between the allegory and building capacity in schools today.
4. Reflect on your own school and identify ways in which the concept of "building capacity" is being initiated/implemented. How is your principal involved in the capacity-building process?
5. What specific leadership practices, as related to capacity building, can Principal Paul Reven of L. E. White School initiate? How? By what means? [Hint: Consider the listing of recommendations as noted in the chapter section, "The Top 11 Capacity-Building Tools."]
6. Why would a principal be predisposed to "share" the school leadership role? Reflect again on the "Shared Leadership" section of chapter 3. Explain in detail.

Chapter 8

Daily Step #8

Self-Reflect, Understand the Power and Problems with Social Networking, Protect Against Cyberbullying, and Establish Professional Networks

> "Power tends to corrupt and absolute power corrupts absolutely. Great men are almost always bad men, even when they exercise influence and not authority: Still more when you superadd the tendency or the certainty of corruption by authority!" —Lord Acton, 1887

BEING THERE

Ever experienced or heard stories of a bad principal, an egotistical principal, a principal who bullies others, or a weak principal? Probably yes to at least one of the noted. Sadly, some principals put their own self-interests ahead of their schools. Others may not be invested or as deeply as would be expected. One assistant principal related a story of the principal at his school:

> The principal at our school was rarely on the campus and instead always attending meetings at the district office. There were times when our principal missed events at school and our leadership team was left scrambling to cover for his absence. The faculty and staff were aware that our principal had greater ambitions at central office, but his lack of visibility and presence created an atmosphere where we were always cynical of him and any of his initiatives. One of our exceptional teachers stated the one thought of many: "With him as leader, school life, well, there is just no support!"

Principals must understand the image that they project and how they are viewed by the school personnel. Absent principals are often viewed as not doing their job or not running the school, or perceived as a bad or weak leader.

The principal's actions or inactions will project an image that can be interpreted in a variety of ways. School personnel may not be aware of all the aspects of a principal's actions but will make assumptions. Perceptions can readily become reality, at least in the minds of some personnel. Principals also have to make decisions about what information to make available to personnel. This, too, can cloud an already murky situation, especially if faculty and staff feel left out or ignored.

Daily, successful principals ensure that school personnel are aware of the administrative schedule. It is not uncommon for principals to attend meetings at the district level, meet with community members, and so on. Having school personnel aware of what is happening with school leadership can go a long way toward ensuring that rumors do not get started. Teachers understand that administrative duties and responsibilities will take a principal off campus. However, teachers also have an expectation that a principal will have a strong on-campus visible presence and always place the school first. Successful principals are aware of how important the physical presence of the school leader is to campus personnel.

CONFIDENCE VS. EGO

Accepting the principalship role requires significant drive, focus, and confidence. But there is a fine line between confidence and ego. Chapter 5 addressed the role of the principal and exploring their ideological and educational beliefs. A principal's ideological and educational beliefs are tied to confidence and ego. It is very important that principals self-reflect on their ego and confidence levels. Principals must recognize that ego prevents success (Jones, 2017). Becoming a principal is a great accomplishment, and it denotes recognition of hard work and commitment. School personnel understand that part of a principal's job is to project confidence. A healthy appreciation of "self" is important. However, to be successful, a principal must be wary of being the solitary and isolated decision-maker. There's a fine line between confidence and ego. Successful principals avoid crossing this line!

SELF-REFLECTION

Self-reflection is a key component of a successful principalship (recall chapter 4 and how successful principals incorporate self-reflection as an approach to the workday). Successful principals carefully consider each administrative role and responsibility. Successful principals take time to reflect upon which of the numerous principal roles are being sacrificed or lost, and where the school leader needs to focus more attention.

Self-reflection refers to making meaning of personal actions as well as inactions. Self-reflection allows a principal to sort through daily personal experiences with the objective of considering different possible interpretations and thus, creating a better way of understanding the meaning and significance of professional life (Porter, 2017). Successful principals use self-reflection to support individual growth which lends itself to being a stronger leader.

School leaders frequently have difficulty making time for self-reflection. Some principals simply do not know how to self-reflect. Self-reflection requires a principal to address activities that are not typical to administrative behavior and thinking (such as slowing down, being curious, and accepting uncertainty). However, self-reflection leads to clearer insights and solutions (Porter, 2017). Self-reflection can tax a principal because it demands a certain degree of vulnerability and often causes personal discomfort while trying to come to grips with the meaning of ideas and beliefs.

Successful principals establish daily self-reflection practices. Successful principals reflect upon specific issues such as: 1) identifying key concerns or questions; 2) reflecting back to recall similar situations and solutions; 3) setting up a time in a quiet place; 4) talking aloud to better hear inner thoughts; 6) taking notes; 7) practicing relaxed breathing; and 8) placing what has been learned into practice.

Self-reflection also helps a principal to more efficiently and effectively process daily achievements. Successful principals ask themselves questions such as:

1) Was I prepared for today?
2) Did I achieve today's objectives?
3) What did I do well and what made it effective?
4) What behaviors or actions can I improve upon?
5) How do I achieve further improvement?
6) What did I learn today from others? and
7) What did others learn from me today?

Self-reflection takes on many forms. It can be meditation to clear the mind. It can be a walk around the school when classes are in session. It can be closing the office door for a personal time out. Self-reflecting at the end of the day will help process events, make sense of decisions, and ultimately organize thoughts for the upcoming day.

Chapter 8

TOMORROW IS ANOTHER DAY

Chapter 3 touched upon the range of problems that principals face daily. Looking beyond today requires an exploration of what tomorrow brings! Events from one day can impact following days. Problems can multiply and must be dealt with. At times, principals are called upon to address issues after school hours. Certain issues are ongoing, others are solvable then and now, yet all interrupt whatever plans have been made.

"Tomorrow is another day" is the last line in Margaret Mitchell's *Gone with the Wind* (1936). Tomorrow alludes to an individual who is experiencing a difficult day, and serves as a reminder that a new day is coming and is always filled with new opportunities. Naturally, not all problems simply disappear overnight. To think so is idealistic. Reality requires a principal to recognize that the old problems must be resolved as new problems will always emerge before the next school day begins. Such is life as a school leader. Successful principals welcome each day with an awareness that there will be events that will flow into the next day and sometimes into days thereafter!

Daily issues, problems, and interactions can make school personnel anxious or frustrated and certainly, conflict can arise Additionally, principals may feel under attack or challenged, or just due to a particularly bad day. It would be easy to suggest "counting to ten," or advising that a principal must be in control of any and every situation. These typical recommendations may be "pie in the sky" solutions or not at all pertinent as principals find themselves caught up in the moment.

How does a successful principal handle such situations? The answer involves forward thinking or reading relative to the ongoing issue or at the very least, reading the mood of a room. Successful principals set the parameters for potentially difficult, if not explosive issues. Successful principals acknowledge opposing views and ask those with opposing views to collaboratively seek and develop solutions.

Successful principals collect and weigh the "pros and cons" of every situation and serve ready to delve into why certain individuals are staunchly in opposition to potential solutions. The very best principals address such opposition and advise the opponents that the issue may not be addressed immediately but will definitely be revisited. Successful principals always follow up and revisit situations where opposing issues come into consideration and then ascertain whether a gap can be bridged.

Self-reflection can aid in bridging differences. However, if self-reflection brings only a one-sided resolution, then lingering frustration can derail progress. Successful principals ensure progress by having colleagues who have opposing views fully realize their concerns are applicable to informing process as well as progress. Oppositional views can wear on a school leader.

However, successful principals plan and meet with colleagues who have contrasting perspectives to better learn and enhance the growth and development of the entire learning community.

Recall that the notion of "tomorrow is another day" is the consideration that every day breeds a new beginning. Some principals view the beginning of each new day as starting anew with a clean slate. Successful principals ensure that frustrations and anger from previous days do not interfere with the progress of the coming day. Once again, this process is tied to time of self-reflection and to making meaning of past events. Successful principals approach each day with a new sense of interest, commitment, and a positive attitude.

EQUALITY AND EQUITY

Principals working with students of color must be aware of the historical inequities that persist and play out in education. Successful principals need to be knowledgeable about the inequities that marginalized students face in schools (such as students with disabilities, LGBQTIA, students of color, religious affiliation, the disenfranchised, and so on). Examples of everyday life inequities include suspensions (Loveless, 2017; U.S. Department of Education Office of Civil Rights, 2014) such as the school-to-prison pipeline (Goetz, 2019).

Students of color, students with disabilities, and LGBQTIA are also suspended at a higher rate than their White counterparts. Principals must recognize that suspensions increase the risk of students dropping out of school and being pushed toward the justice system (Nittle, 2019). Black students, even at the preschool level, face severe discipline. Successful principals recognize that minority students are:

- Less likely to be identified as gifted;
- Less likely to have highly qualified teachers (or teachers representing their race, ethnicity, or culture), as noted in chapter 7;
- Most likely to attend schools with greater police presence;
- Almost certain to face micro-aggressions such as greater criticisms for hair styles (such as braids or natural), clothing, and food smells; and
- Most likely to meet increased segregation (Nittle, 2019).

Principals must be aware that these disparities are institutionally embedded within a school system.

The United States Declaration of Independence proudly declares "We hold these truths to be self-evident, that all men are created equal" (United States,

1776). The 13th, 14th, and 15th Amendments in the United States Constitution address the matter of abolished slavery, allow for equal protection, and establish the right for all to vote. However, this focus on equality has continued to obscure the inequities that exist in our schools.

It is important that school leaders understand the differences between equality and equity. Equality is the belief that everyone should be treated with the same expectations, having the same status, rights, and opportunities. Equality is embedded within American society and is celebrated along with life, liberty, and the pursuit of happiness. However, this chapter focus is on the issues of equity.

Equity refers to meeting the individual needs of marginalized students. Equity seeks to address students who tend to fall through the cracks. Competing conservative views perceive equity as distributing funding to specific groups at the expense of others (Friedman, 2018). Equality assumes that all students (racial and ethnic groups, social class, ability, and gender) should receive the same education (Jordan, 2010).

Successful principals understand that equity recognizes that there have been dramatic increases in diversity such as ethnic, cultural, and language differences. The focus on equity aims to eradicate racial discrimination in schools. The objective is to embed equalized educational opportunities through culturally relevant pedagogies by recognizing the diversity of the student body (Jordan, 2010).

The focus on accountability and specifically meritocracy has meant that schools focus strongly on student and classroom scores based upon coursework as measured by state testing, participation, and attendance. Meritocracy dictates that the education system forces all students (marginalized groups in particular) to fit into a hierarchal structure (Mungal, 2020b). This hierarchal structure is connected to institutional bias as discussed in chapter 5. Successful principals need to embrace equity, ensuring that marginalized groups are uplifted and given opportunities that even the playing field.

IN THE ERA OF SOCIAL MEDIA AND SOCIAL NETWORKING

Social media includes apps and websites that allow users to share content such as information, ideas, pictures, music, and so on. This phenomenon is termed social networking. Social media can be a useful tool that allows teachers to expand the ways that they teach. It can support the sharing of information between districts, schools, parents, and students. Social media can enhance lessons and increase student participation. Social networking and social media permit teachers to share information with students in creative ways. Social media aids students to become more proficient with technological skills.

Principals must understand the power and problems that come with social networking and social media use in schools. Successful principals plan for and initiate school policies to help address any potential problems. One of the most important issues is making teachers aware of current social networking and media apps and tools such as Facebook, Twitter, Instagram, Snapchat, WhatsApp, Pinterest, Tumblr, Reddit—the listing goes on and on. There are also social networks for many special interests. For example, there are niche social networks for gamers such as Discord or for music such as Musical.ly.

New apps are being developed every day, and the casual observer may not know or notice these new apps. A quick look through Google Store or Apple's App Store reveals several hundred social networking and social media apps. Take a moment to check.

Interestingly, the first adapters to technology and to social networking and media tend to be students. Asking a group of students which social apps they use will garner a list of apps that fly under the radar of regular usage but may be very popular with students. How will a principal keep track of these constant upgrades in technology? Sometimes it can be as simple as having conversations with students or communicating with teachers. Successful principals must consider providing professional development to faculty and staff so all can understand the impact of social networking and be aware of signs of cyberbullying.

SOCIAL NETWORKING AND CYBERBULLYING

While there are positive uses for social media in the classroom and in personal life, there is also a dark side that has caused national headlines. Stories of cyberbullying has also led to physical, emotional, and sexual harassment (Leemis, Espelage, Mercer Kollar & Davis, 2018), anxiety, low self-esteem, depression (Kowalski & Limber, 2013) and suicide (Hinduja & Patchin, 2010) all of which can impact academics. Ten- to fourteen-year-old girls, LGBQTIA students, youth with disabilities, and introverted or shy students are at a greater risk for suicide (National Voices for Equality, Education, and Enlightenment, 2019).

The U.S. government (2019) provides an excellent website to help the general public and educators, in particular, to better understand cyberbullying at www.stopbullying.gov. This site provides prevention and resources to help prevent all types of bullying. Moreover, the New York State Education Department (2016) provides educators with insight and other information to prevent bullying at http://www.p12.nysed.gov/dignityact/documents/PreventBullyingInYourSchool_Nov2016.pdf. With the rise in bullying and cyberbullying, these websites must be essential reading for all educators.

BULLYING AND CYBERBULLYING PREVENTION

District leaders and campus principals must have strong social media policies to ensure flexibility but still provide protection against cyberbullying. District principals must bring together stakeholders including students and parents, as well as connect with lawyers to create specific recommendations. These policies must encourage learning but ensure student privacy. Policies must focus on conduct and behavior and be accessible. Yet, school districts need to be wary of overregulating and recognize how the issues of off-campus actions can impact schooling. Policies must have clear rules, expectations, and guidelines (Bendici, 2019).

Additional recommendations that principals must consider include:

1. Establishing zero-tolerance bullying policies. Principals, however, must recognize that such policies allow for limited flexibility and assume all episodes are equal.
2. Bringing together stakeholders to develop guidelines. Successful principals ensure that the policies and guidelines are regularly reviewed and updated.
3. Providing professional development and resources for teachers to instruct students about all forms of bullying. This must include discussions on consequences.
4. Reinforcing an anti-bully agenda and emphasizing good behavior.
5. Investing in peer counseling for all students relative to instances of bullying.
6. Providing more counselors to better ensure a safe space for support and working with victims and bullies. Some recommendations include supporting reconciliation and continued monitoring process (Thompson, 2019).

Successful principals include parents in decision-making procedures since the parents have more authority with discipline. Parents, teachers, and other stakeholders must relay to students how to incorporate technology in responsible ways. Students must understand that their posts and pictures on social media are there forever, and that postings can be identified through IP addresses (Thompson, 2019). Parents must monitor their children's technology and cell-phone usage. Daily, successful principals take into consideration all of the above information to help prevent all types of bullying.

INFORMAL AND FORMAL NETWORKS

The principal has many roles and responsibilities. As the school leader, the principal provides direction, enforces policies, hires and evaluates personnel, manages the budget, builds community relationships, evaluates curriculum, analyzes student scores, and so much more. The principalship is still viewed as an isolated position of leadership. Successful principals understand that a strong network can help remove the isolation by creating a support system.

Formal and informal networks help to build a support system that a successful principal can tap into. Though written for new principals, Reyna's (2017) work has implications for all principals. Formal networks usually begin with the promotion to the principalship with school districts providing service and training. Experienced principals act as mentors to the new incoming principals.

Theoretically, these formal networks are geared to help new principals navigate their first year, have them engage with experienced principals, and have support from the school district itself. The mentorship permits a principal to be socialized to the district policies, procedures, regulations, and practices (Reyna, 2017). Additionally, the mentorship is intended to be a moral and ethical ideological guide. While many mentors will be engaged and supportive, Reyna (2017) reports that experienced principals may not be as available as the district intends as these principals have limited time as a result of their own campus expectations, responsibilities, and demands.

The formal network provides a more official approach to issues in the schools. It is vital to maintain a connection with the formalized networks to ensure that principal approaches are professional and that new principals remain in good stead with colleagues, mentors, and district personnel.

Informal networks can benefit and support principals as well. This support comes from allies such as principal colleagues, assistant principals, instructional coaches, other leadership members, and even campus counselors (Reyna, 2017). Informal networks will also consist of peers from university or district leadership programs, master's degree peers, and new principals who enter into the principalship at the same time. Informal networks often begin at formalized meetings or from casual connections with other principals. Informal networks are about relationship building with colleagues who are sharing the same principal experiences. Such informal relationships allow for greater freedom to discuss concerns with colleagues who will be not only understanding, but supportive.

Formal and informal networks are important for principals to succeed. The very best principals utilize the formal and informal support system to gain knowledge, discuss issues, refine ideas, and gather unique or different perspectives.

Both formal and informal networks permit principals to learn from peers and mentors. Successful principals understand the pressures and scrutiny of the position, which can be alleviated by communication with peers. Successful principals are able to share their experiences to help others and to also gain insight into current issues. It is an opportunity to observe if incidents are independent or if there are district-wide trends.

Successful principals also recognize that family and friends play an important role in their success. Principals need to have the support of family and friends as the job can take over one's life. The hours are long, the stakes are high, and failures often overshadow successes. Family and friends offer a respite from the pressures of the school and allow a principal to reconnect to the person, not the position. Principals must differentiate between their public and personal lives. Remember, self-reflect each day before going home. Avoid bringing home those daily stressors and frustrations!

SOCIAL MOVEMENTS AND CRITICAL THINKING

Successful principals recognize that education is a microcosm of society and as society has entered into an age of social movements, so must schooling. There have been movements throughout history, such as the Abolitionist Movement, the Temperance Movement, the Women's Rights Movement, the Civil Rights Movement, and the Equal Rights Movement and associated Amendment, just to name a few. These movements have radically altered the very fabric of the nation, signaling a changing social consciousness.

More recent social movements include Occupy Wall Street (OWS), Black Lives Matter, Me Too Movement, Times Up, the Deferred Action for Child Arrivals (DACA), the Development, Relief, and Education for Alien Minors Act (DREAM ACT), the Gun Control Movement, along with the most recent immigration and refugee rights movement (Callahan, 2018). Conservative social movements such as the Tea Party and the evangelical movement, as well as a rise in racial movements have occurred. With access to the Internet, students of all ages now have the same right of entry to this information and so much more.

Perhaps because of the Internet and social media, students have become more connected to world events, while at the same time being less engaged in social interactions. Principals sometimes forget their own experiences as students and even student activists. As principals grow older, and with the passage of time, such a lapse in memory or disconnection leads school leaders to question the motives of the young. However, as witnessed time and time again, students can and will become engaged, critical of, and aware of social inequities.

Principals and learning communities must become aware of past, immediate, and newly conceived social movements. Principals, too, must walk a fine line between encouragement and caution. Access to the news and other media information can be both enlightening and exciting, but without strong critical thinking skills, students will not always question content. Students will be exposed to opinions presented in the form of factual data (the truth) as well as information that has been altered for political advantage. Remember, paying critical attention is essential to avoiding falling victim to what could very well be deceitful disinformation, if not all out, blatant lies.

Successful principals must encourage not only the teaching by faculty, but also the development of student critical thinking skills. These skills must continually be reinforced throughout the school years and within and across differing disciplines. The presentation of what is empirical data, as well as fact and opinion, has become greatly obscured. The teaching of critical thinking skills is beneficial:

1. For analyzing and evaluating data;
2. For being skeptical in terms of properly questioning and analyzing received information;
3. For emphasizing evidence-based thinking instead of emotionally-oriented decisions;
4. For recognizing assumptions and biases;
5. For acquiring understanding, knowledge, and truth through critical analyses as well as self-reflection; and
6. For building independent reflection and analysis as well as critical thinking skills.

Most important, critical thinking better ensures that students effectively and appropriately navigate information on the Internet, as well as in their day-to-day interactions with school work and even personal interests.

Successful principals ensure the creation and advancement of professional development for teachers. Such professional development must prepare teachers to successfully engage students, instructionally, in becoming critical thinkers. Successful principals who invest in the professional training of faculty and staff must either lead the sessions or select qualified experts from the school district or education schools. If principals are not the professional development presenters/leaders, they must be present (for the entire professional development session), engaged, and actively interacting.

An important resource for principals and teachers: Teachthought (2019) provides 25 critical thinking resources at www.teachthought.com/critical-thinking/25-resources-for-teaching-critical-thinking/.

ALTERNATIVE TEACHERS WITH ALTERNATIVE TRAINING

Alternative teacher preparation programs have grown by leaps and bounds. At one time they made up a very small part of the teachers being produced. However, within the last decade, alternative teacher preparation programs have become the norm. Most teachers are trained within schools of education connected to colleges and universities. Alternative teacher preparation programs can be stand-alone programs such as Relay Graduate School (Mungal, 2019), or various city, state, or national alternative programs such as Teach For America (Mungal, 2016).

As alternative routes into teaching expand, principals must not only employ, but also work with teachers produced by such programs. There are pros and cons to alternatively trained teachers. Programs such as Teach For America have proclaimed that they recruit successful graduates from highly selective colleges and universities (Mungal, 2012). However, research indicates that such programs train teachers to teach a highly prescriptive model, meaning that there is no room for differentiated learning styles that cater to the variety of student learning levels (Mungal, 2015; 2019).

Successful principals are aware that teacher training can and will impact student learning, whether it be positive or negative. Professional development can aid alternatively trained teachers, as well as all teachers to be more responsive to the differentiated learning styles of students. Successful principals recognize this factor and, therefore, monitor and encourage alternatively trained teachers to expand their teaching capacity and delivery.

LEADERSHIP IN A CHANGING WORLD

With the changing demographics across the United States and the world, more and more individuals of color and marginalized groups are entering the education profession. In some instances, these groups will represent the communities around their schools. In other instances, minority teachers may still be expanding, if not breaking, barriers as they enter into schools with homogeneous populations.

Successful principals support changing demographics, individuals of color, and marginalized groups into the teaching profession. Welcoming teachers with different backgrounds, cultures, ethnicities, and abilities can provide role models for students, and for teachers, and further serves to break down long-held prejudices and stereotypes. Successful principals daily create a support system for teachers that considers not only their teaching skills but also how said teachers can positively impact students and the learning community. Remember, equity must be extended to teachers as well as students.

Finally, successful principals encourage and mentor teachers of all backgrounds. Skilled minority teachers, if not supported by principals, can very well fall through the cracks due to systemic and institutional biases. Successful principals mentor teachers to navigate the system. Successful principals utilize the various cultural backgrounds, ethnic identities, and diverse abilities that marginalized teachers bring into a school.

FINAL THOUGHTS

Successful principals understand the image they project as well as how they are perceived by the learning community. Daily, these principals ensure personnel are aware of what is happening at the school-site level by maintaining a strong on-campus visible presence. The very best principals always place the school community first.

Successful principals possess an essential drive, focus, and confidence. They also recognize that ego can prevent success. While a healthy appreciation of "self" is important, successful principals understand there is a fine line between confidence and ego and thus avoid crossing this line into the less than acceptable and appreciated "ego" lane.

Successful principals incorporate self-reflection into their daily professional life to create a better method of understanding the meaning and significance of the profession which, in turn, serves to support personal growth and development. Self-reflection permits successful principals to identify key professional concerns, to recall similar situations and solutions, and to place what has been learned into practice.

Successful principals know that daily issues, problems, and conflicts create an anxious, if not frustrated, learning community. To handle such, successful principals accurately "read" campus personnel and delve into certain issues and/or problems—to include those created by individuals with opposing viewpoints.

Successful principals recognize the difference between equity and equality. They work to meet the varied individual needs of marginalized students—students of color and/or diverse differences such as those related to ethnicity, culture, and language. Successful principals embrace equity, ensure marginalized students are uplifted, and provide academic, social, and emotional opportunities that serve to even the educational playing field. These principals make it their daily objective to eradicate educational measures and methods that further marginalize student groups.

Successful principals understand the power and problems associated with social networking and social media in schools. The very best principals provide and lead professional development to faculty and staff so all can recognize and instructionally adapt to the impact of social networking.

Successful principals engage all members of the learning community in the prevention of bullying and cyberbullying by establishing zero-tolerance bullying policies; by providing professional development and anti-bullying resources for teachers in their instruction of students; and by investing in additional counselors and student support.

Finally, successful principals develop both formal and informal networks as a means of gaining a deeper understanding of the leadership role and acquiring supportive relationships. The very best principals develop mentorships with novice school leaders helping guide them morally, ethically, instructionally, and professionally. These relationships build comradery and lasting friendships, and allow for opportunities to garner further knowledge, discuss relevant personal and professional issues—free from judgment— refine ideas, develop unique or differing perspectives, and release job-related stress and professional tensions.

DISCUSSION QUESTIONS

1. A general research-based conclusion is that attributes that tend to have a negative connotation in our culture—being egotistical, for example—are adverse factors in relation to group dynamics, productivity, morale, and cohesiveness. What are the attributes of an egotistical leader? Identify, and then explain why such behavioral attributes are indicators of an individual who will make an unsuccessful school principal.
2. How will school leaders who engage in self-reflection be better, if not successful, principals? Explain.
3. Explain the difference between equality and equity. Which of the two defined terms better serves students, teachers, and school leaders? Be specific in your answer.
4. Principals, as well as all educators, live and work in an era of social media and social networking. Identify the positive aspects of the mediums, along with the negative. How can a school principal be best prepared to handle both social media and social networking?
5. Reference the chapter section entitled "Bullying and Cyberbullying Prevention." Of the six recommendations that principals must consider relative to the topic, which three are absolutely critical guidelines for successful school leadership and student safety and security?

6. Why are informal and formal networks essential to principal success? Of the two types of networking, which one best helps in terms of principal success? Explain.
7. Critical thinking skills must be strongly encouraged by principals at the school-site level. Which three of the six indicators of beneficial reasons to teach critical thinking skills best serve students? Be specific in your answer.

CASE STUDY APPLICATION—CYBERSTALKED

Penelope, a 14-year-old female student at Harbor Bridge Middle School, happened to be one tech-savvy teenager. Penelope spent a great deal of time social networking. Specifically, she was drawn to an online social media and social networking service, as well as a multimedia messaging app that promoted a fun and easy way to talk and share photos, and a video-sharing website—all very popular with teenagers today. Penelope's parents, with whom she had a rather estranged relationship, were far from tech-savvy. Yes, both her mother and father possessed laptops that they utilized for work and to monitor emails, but that was just about the depth of their digital capabilities.

Penelope, a highly-intelligent teenager, was described by one of her friends, Brock, as being too smart for her own good. Brock, too, was tech-savvy but regularly erred on the side of caution. Brock loved technology, but expressed a level of wariness regarding social media. Brock had an innate understanding of both the advantages and disadvantages of certain websites and differing cell-phone apps such as those that prescribed violent tendencies (gathering, crafting, and combating; kill or be killed).

Brock's parents, like their son, were extremely tech-savvy and had regular digitally-oriented conversations with their son. These parent-to-son talks related to the horrors of cyberstalking, cyberbullying, cyberghosting, and even cyberpower gaming computers, as well as discussions regarding the benefits and safety of cyber-awareness and cyber-security. Recently, prior to what became known at Harbor Bridge School as the "cyber-disaster," Brock had a lengthy conversation with Penelope regarding cyber-awareness.

Brock shared with Penelope that she was asking for trouble as a result of what Brock called her "digital obsession" and "techno-addiction." Penelope happened, at the time, to be livestreaming the video game she was playing. Brock knew that livestreaming was a power-adrenalin enhancer as well as a dangerous combination of epinephrine stimuli and perilously addictive vulnerability. Penelope played on and the price she was to pay would be steep!

The Rub: Therein Lies the Trip!

Penelope fell hard for Griffith. He was a 14-year-old classmate. Tall for his age, flowing blonde hair, brown eyes, a bright flashing smile, a great teenage male physique, and an outgoing personality, Griffith was spellbinding to the doe-eyed gaze of Penelope. She had a huge crush on this middle school hunk. Griffith knew his charms and readily used, if not abused, them.

Griffith spoke to Penelope, herself more physically developed than her female peers, one day during third-period math class. Griffith told Penelope that he would go out with her if she went to the restroom, took a photo of herself without any of her clothes on and sent it to him before math class was over. Griffith was specific in what he wanted to see in the photo and convinced Penelope that if she immediately shared the photo via a certain cell-phone app that said photo would be automatically discarded once disseminated by the sender (Penelope) and received by the intended recipient (Griffith).

Penelope, emotionally immature, was convinced to send the photo—which she took and sent in the girl's restroom during the math class period. What Griffith failed to confide in Penelope was his intention to create a screenshot and save the photo—which he did. Griffith later electronically shared Penelope's self-created child pornographic snapshot with several of his male friends. Penelope never realized the double-cross until three days later when a girlfriend told her of this male-to-males digital activity. What Penelope didn't recognize was that this particular episode was just the beginning of hazards to come!

During an online chat a few days later, Penelope was enticed by a 52-year-old man to meet him at a convenience store near her home. The man needed a back rub and stated he'd pay Penelope $25.00 if she helped him out. Penelope was already planning a getaway from her tiresome parents with whom she was steadily rebellious. The cash would definitely come in handy. Later, she met the man, in his car, on a secluded side of the convenience store. Penelope asked for the cash up-front. The man obliged. After the back rub, the man began to unzip his pants. Penelope wisely and speedily retreated from the vehicle and ran home.

Another "creeper"—a cyberstalker—was also engaging Penelope via her online social networking account. The male, 35-years-of-age, was able to convince Penelope to come to Mexico and meet up with him. He would show her a fun time on the Pacific coastline. Penelope used the previously gained $25.00 to obtain a bus ticket for the trip—a trip which turned out to be far from long enough to reach the United States/Mexico border. At the end of the first leg of her bus excursion and out of money, Penelope schemed a female bus ticket agent into giving her a ticket for the reminder of the way. The adult attendant fell for the well-conceived con as Penelope told the ticket agent that her purse had been stolen, along with her remaining savings.

By this time, several days had passed since Penelope first ran away from home. Her parents frantically contacted local authorities who, in turn, brought in the Federal Bureau of Investigation (FBI). The FBI took over Penelope's web account and with a great deal of zeal, skill, and luck, the cyber-squad tracked the young female victim to a small bus stop near the pre-determined border crossing point. Penelope was rescued from any and all harm. A daring feat, evading what would have been an alarming, if not deadly, consequence!

Application Questions

1. The case study examined a negative aspect of social media and social networking. Reflect back to the related chapter section and identify the positive aspects of the phenomenon. Include in your response your own positive interactions, from an educational and leadership perspective, with the medium.
2. Identify what you believe or have experienced relative to the power and problems of social networking and social media—again, from an educational perspective.
3. What, if any, are the disciplinary repercussions for the actions of Griffith as identified in the case study? For Penelope? Support your conclusions with specific campus regulations and district policies. Do real student "Griffiths" and "Penelopes" exist in schools? What's a principal to do? Explain.
4. Which of the policy considerations for bullying and cyberbullying prevention, as identified in the chapter, best apply to this particular case study? Explain why.
5. Why do you think first adapters to technology and to social networking and social media tend to be middle school students, much like Penelope, Brock, and Griffith? Explain your reasoning. What's a principal and team to do in preventing students from engaging in cyberbullying as well as the "dark side" of social networking and media? What does the empirical research reveal?
6. Step into the role of principal at Harbor Bridge Middle School. How would you and your leadership team (teachers and counselors included) work with Penelope upon her return to school, following her social media- and networking-related ordeal? Provide detailed and relevant advice, as well as specific steps or measures.

References

Arnold, M. (2015). What is reality therapy? Retrieved from https://www.crchealth.com/types-of-therapy/reality-therapy/
Arnstein, S. R. (1969). A ladder of participation. *Journal of the American Institute of Planners, 35*, 216-233.
Avolio, B. J., Howell, J. M., & Sosik, J. J. (1999). A funny thing happened on the way to the bottom line: Humor as a moderator of leadership style effects. *Academy of Management Journal 42*(2), 219-227.
AZ Quotes. (2015a). *Cultural diversity quotes*. Retrieved July 2, 2019, from https://www.azquotes.com/quotes/topics/cultural-diversity.html
AZ Quotes. (2015b). *Grenville Kleiser good humor*. Retrieved February 10, 2019, from https://www.google.com/search?q=Humor+quotes&tbm=isch&source=hp&sa=X&ved=2ahUKEwiryPu1ua_gAhUSEawKHWn2Bz8QsAR6BAgEEAE&biw=1366&bih=626#imgrc=LiL_CULKxe1XDM:
Bambrick-Santoyo, P. (2018). *Leverage leadership 2.0: A practical guide to building exceptional schools*. San Francisco, CA: Jossey-Bass.
Banks, R. R., Eberhardt, J. L., & Ross, L. (2006). Discrimination and implicit bias in a racially unequal society. *California Law Review, 94*(4), 1169-1190.
Batterson, M. (2006). *In a pit with a lion on a snowy day: How to survive and thrive when opportunity roars*. New York, NY: Multnomah Books.
Baumeister, R. F., Campbell, J. D., Krueger, J. I., & Vohs, K. D. (2003). Does high self-esteem cause better performance, interpersonal success, happiness, or healthier lifestyles? *American Psychological Society 4*(1), 1-44.
Bell Leadership Institute. (2012). *Bell Leadership study finds humor gives leaders the edge*. Retrieved February 11, 2019, from https://www.bellleadership.com/humor-gives-leaders-edge/
Bendici, R. (2019). How to create K12 social media policy. Retrieved July 18, 2019, from https://districtadministration.com/how-to-create-k12-social-media-policy/
Bennett, N. A. (2019). 6 ways to prevent racism in school. *Kickboard Blog*. Retrieved from https://www.kickboardforschools.com/blog/post/6-ways-to-prevent-racism-in-schools

Berra, Y., & Kaplan, D. (2002). *When you come to a fork in the road, take it! Inspiration and wisdom from one of baseball's greatest heroes.* New York, NY: Hachette Group Books.

Berra, Y. (2010). *The Yogi book: I really didn't say everything I said.* New York, NY: Workman Publishing Company.

Bharthvajan, R. (2019). *Organization culture and climate.* Retrieved June 8, 2019, from http://www.rroij.com/open-access/organizational-culture-and-climate-.php?aid=46147

Blackman, A. (2018). What is unconscious bias? + top strategies to help avoid it. *Diversity.* Retrieved from https://business.tutsplus.com/tutorials/what-is-unconscious-bias--cms-31455

Blad, E., & Harwin, A. (2017). Black students more likely to be arrested at school. Retrieved June 14, 2019, from https://www.edweek.org/ew/articles/2017/01/25/black-students-more-likely-to-be-arrested.html

Bowen, N. (2002). *Ralph Nader: A man with a mission.* Minneapolis, MN: Millbrook Press.

Brainy Quote. (2001-2019a). *Dwight D. Eisenhower diary quotes.* Retrieved February 10, 2019, from https://www.brainyquote.com/topics/diary

Brainy Quote. (2001-2019b). *Mark Twain quotes.* Retrieved February 10, 2019, from https://www.brainyquote.com/authors/mark_twain

Brainy Quote. (2001-2019c). *Charlie Chaplin quotes.* Retrieved February 10, 2019, from https://www.brainyquote.com/authors/charlie_chaplin

Brown, K. M., & Shaked, H. (2018). *Preparing future leaders for social justice: Bridging theory and practice through a transformative andragogy.* Lanham, MD: Rowman & Littlefield.

Buchanan, L. (2018). *Why funny leaders are better leaders.* Retrieved February 11, 2019, from https://www.inc.com/leigh-buchanan/everyone-loves-a-funny-leader.html

Callahan, M. (2018). *#MeToo, #BlackLivesMatter, #NoBanNoWall: Social Movements Likely to Dominate 2018.* Retrieved July 12, 2019, from https://news.northeastern.edu/2018/01/12/metoo-blacklivesmatter-nobannowall-social-movements-likely-to-dominate-2018/

Campbell, R. (2018). *Sense of humor: Great leadership characteristic.* Retrieved February 11, 2019, from https://www.robcampbellleadership.com/blog/2018/6/27/sense-of-humor-a-great-leadership-characteristic

Castro, V. (2017). 4 things we can do to minimize implicit biases. Retrieved, June 22, 2019, from https://www.diversitycouncil.org/single-post/2017/01/10/From-Vangies-Desk-4-Things-We-Can-Do-to-Minimize-Implicit-Biases

Caulfield, J., Kidd, S., & Kocher, T. (2000). Brain-based instruction in action. *Educational Leadership, 58*(3), 62-65.

Center for Teaching and Learning. (2019). *Engaging students in learning.* Retrieved July 21, 2019, from https://www.washington.edu/teaching/teaching-resources/engaging-students-in-learning/

Cesar E. Chavez Foundation – United Farm Workers. (2019). *Education of the heart – Cesar Chavez in his own words.* Los Angeles, CA: Author.

Community Relations Services Toolkit for Policing. (n.d.). *Understanding bias: A resource guide.* Washington, DC: U.S. Department of Justice Retrieved July 21, 2019, from https://www.justice.gov/crs/file/836431/download

Connolly, M. (2008). The courage of educational leaders. *Principal* (May/June), 68.

Cowen, A. (2018). 8 Leadership Styles: Which One Are You? *Leadership Skills.* Retrieved July 21, 2019, from https://aboutleaders.com/8-leadership-styles-one/#gs.gdxxz6

Cray, M., & Weiler, S. C. (2011). Principal preparedness: Superintendent perceptions of new principals. *Journal of School Leadership, 21*(6), 927-945.

Desravines, J., Aquino, J., & Fenton, B. (2016). *Breakthrough principals: A step-by-step guide to building stronger schools.* San Francisco, CA: Jossey-Bass.

DuFour, R., & Mattos, M. (2013). How do principals really improve schools? *The Principalship, 70*(7), 34-40.

Eckert, J. (2018). *Leading together: Teachers and administrators improving student outcomes.* Thousand Oaks, CA: Corwin.

Fazio, R. (2018). *Lead with laughter: How humor can positively transform a work environment.* Retrieved February 12, 2019, from https://www.forbes.com/sites/forbescoachescouncil/2018/08/10/lead-with-laughter-how-humor-can-positively-transform-a-work-enviroment/#48d86f965c94

Fiarman, S. E. (2016). Unconscious bias: When good intentions aren't enough. *Educational Leadership, 74*(3), 10-15.

Friedman, J. (2018). Defining equity vs. equality in education. *Shaped.* Retrieved July 13, 2019, from https://www.hmhco.com/blog/defining-equity-in-your-school-district

Fullan, M. (2014). *The principal: Three keys to maximizing impact.* San Francisco, CA: Jossey-Bass.

Fullan, M. (2003). *The moral imperative of school leadership.* Thousand Oaks, CA: Corwin.

Gibson, L. (2003). Leadership with laughter. *Urologic Nursing, 23*(5), 364.

Goetz, S. (2019). School-to-prison pipeline and its infestation in the Black and Brown communities. *Augberg Honors Review, 12*(Article 1).

Goldsmith, L. M. (2019). *Take a hike! Take a long walk on a short pier – but don't fall into the deep!* Unpublished interview. Department of Educational Leadership and Foundations, The University of Texas at El Paso, El Paso, TX.

Google Quotes. (2019). *Organized quotes.* Retrieved February 2, 2019, from https://www.google.com/search?q=Organized+quotes&tbm=isch&source=hp&sa=X&ved=2ahUKEwjqroC226TgAhVE71QKHRtOBegQsAR6BAgEEAE&biw=1366&bih=626#imgrc=txfP1SSEEbJM9M

Guido, M. (2017). 15 Culturally-responsive teaching strategies and examples. Retrieved from https://www.prodigygame.com/blog/culturally-responsive-teaching/

Guthrie, J. W., & Schuermann, P. J. (2010). *Successful school leadership: Planning, politics, performance, and power.* Boston, MA: Pearson Education, Inc.

Hadden, K. (2019). How principals build capacity. Retrieved January 16, 2019, from https://www.teachers.ab.ca/News%20Room/ata%20magazine/Volume%2088/Number%202/Articles/Pages/How%20Principals%20Build%20Capacity.aspx

Hall, P. (2014). How to build teachers' capacity for success. Retrieved January 16, 2019, from http://inservice.ascd.org/how-to-build-teachers-capacity-for-success/

Hall, P., & Simeral, A. (2017). *Creating a culture of reflective practice: Capacity-building for schoolwide success.* Alexandria, VA: Association for Supervision and Curriculum Development (ASCD).

Hall, P., & Simeral, A. (2008). *Building teachers' capacity for success: A collaborative approach for coaches and school leaders.* Alexandria, VA: Association for Supervision and Curriculum Development (ASCD).

Handelsman, J., & Sakraney, N. (2015). *Implicit bias.* Washington, DC: White House Office of Science and Technology Policy Retrieved from https://obamawhitehouse.archives.gov/sites/default/files/microsites/ostp/bias_9-14-15_final.pdf

Harvard Mahoney Neuroscience Institute. (2010). *Humor, laughter, and those aha moments.* Retrieved February 12, 2019, from https://hms.harvard.edu/sites/default/files/HMS_OTB_Spring10_Vol16_No2.pdf

Heller, R. (1998). *Managing change.* New York, NY: DK Publishing, Inc.

Hinduja, S., & Patchin, J. W. (2010). Cyberbullying research summary: Cyberbullying and suicide. Retrieved July 13, 2019, from http://cyberbullying.org/cyberbullying_and_suicide_research_fact_sheet.pdf

Hopper, J., Sowers, S., Brinkley, C. J., Smith, O., & Saarnio, D. (2019). Developing civic-mindedness in middle- and high-school students using service-learning. *Interdisciplinary STEM Teaching & Learning Conference. 14.*

Hoy, A. W., & Hoy, W. K. (2012). *Instructional leadership: A research-based guide to learning in schools.* Boston, MA: Pearson Education, Inc.

Hughes, R. L., Ginnett, R. C., & Curphy, G. J. (2019). *Leadership: Enhancing the lessons of experience, 9th ed.* New York, NY: McGraw-Hill Education.

Indeed Career Guide. (2019). *10 common leadership styles.* Retrieved July 21, 2019, from https://www.indeed.com/career-advice/career-development/10-common-leadership-styles

Jaffe, E. (2010). The psychological study of smiling. Retrieved February 10, 2019, from https://www.psychologicalscience.org/oberver/the-psychological-study-of-smiling

Johnson, A. D. (2016). Principal perceptions of the effectiveness of university educational leadership preparation and professional learning. *NCPEA International Journal of Educational Leadership Preparation, 11*(1), 14-30.

Jones, J. (2017). Get your leadership ego out of the way and empower your students. *Principal Difference.* Retrieved July 10, 2019, from http://blog.nassp.org/2017/12/13/get-your-leadership-ego-out-of-the-way-and-empower-your-students/

Jordan, W. J. (2010). Defining equity: Multiple perspectives to analyzing the performance of diverse learners. *Review of Research in Education, 34*(142), 142-179.

Kowalski, R. M., & Limber, S. P. (2013). Psychological, physical, and academic correlates of cyberbullying and traditional bullying. *Journal of Adolescent Health, 53*(1, Supplement), S13-S20.

Ladson-Billings, G. (1995). Toward a theory of culturally relevant pedagogy. *American Educational Research Journal, 32*(3), 465-491.

Leemis, R. W., Espelage, D. L., Basile, K. C., Mercer Kollar, L. M., & Davis, J. P. (2018). Traditional and cyber bullying and sexual harassment: A longitudinal assessment of risk and protective factors. *Aggressive behavior, 45*(no. 2 (2019)), 181-192.

Loveless, T. (2017). *2017 Brown Center report on American education: Race and school suspensions*. Retrieved July 13, 2019, from Washington, DC: https://www.brookings.edu/research/2017-brown-center-report-part-iii-race-and-school-suspensions/

Lynch, M. (2016). *4 major types of educational leadership*. Retrieved July 21, 2019, from https://www.theedadvocate.org/4-major-types-of-educational-leadership/#

Lyrics.com (2001-2019). *When you're smiling*. Retrieved February 10, 2019, from https://www.lyrics.com/lyric/5778393/Louis+Armstrong/When+You%27re+Smiling+%28The+Whole+World+Smiles+With+You%29

McEwan, E. K. (2005). *How to deal with teachers who are angry, troubled, exhausted, or just plain confused*. Thousand Oaks, CA: Corwin.

McQuerrey, L. (2019). The Advantages of Diverse Ages in the Workplace. Retrieved July 20, 2019, from http://smallbusiness.chron.com/advantages-diverse-ages-workplace-17928html

Martinez, J. I. (2017). *Agent of social capital: An autoethnographic study of a first-time superintendent*. (Ed. D Dissertation), The University of Texas at El Paso, El Paso, TX. Retrieved from https://digitalcommons.utep.edu/dissertations/AAI10686961/

Marzano, R. J., Waters, T., & McNulty, B. A. (2010). *School leadership that works: From research to results*. Alexandria, VA: Association for Supervision and Curriculum Development (ASCD).

Mayo Clinic. (2016). *Stress relief from laughter? It's no joke*. Retrieved February 12, 2019, from https://www.mayoclinic.org/healthy-lifestyle/stress-management/in-depth/stress-relief/art-20044456

Microsoft. (2015). *eLesson: Unconscious bias*. Retrieved July 21, 2019, from https://www.mslearning.microsoft.com/course/72169/launch

Miller, C. M., & Martin, B. N. (2014). Principal preparedness for leading in demographically changing schools. *Educational Management Administration and Leadership*. Retrieved January 24, 2019, from http://journals.sagepub.com/doi/abs/10.1177/1741143213513185

MindTools.com (2019). *How good are your people skills?* Retrieved February 10, 2019, from https://www.mindtools.com/pages/article/newTMM_36.htm

Mitchell, M. (1936). *Gone with the wind*: New York, NY: Macmillan Publishing.

Mitgang, L. D. (2008). *Becoming a leader: Preparing principals for today's schools*. Retrieved July 21, 2019, from New York, NY: https://www.wallacefoundation.org/knowledge-center/Documents/Becoming-a-Leader-Preparing-Principals-for-Todays-Schools.pdf

Morrison, A., White, R., & Van Velsor, E. (1992). *Breaking the glass ceiling*. New York, NY: The Perseus Books Group Publishing Company.

Mungal, A. S. (2020b). Inequities and ethical dilemmas beyond the classroom: Joseph's story. *The Educational Forum* (forthcoming).

Mungal, A. S. (2020, forthcoming). Understanding student-teachers experiences and interactions with K-12 administrators. Submitted to *Educational Administration Quarterly*.

Mungal, A. S. (2019). The emergence of Relay Graduate School. *Issues in Teacher Education, 28*(Number 1, Spring 2019), 52-79.

Mungal, A. S. (2016). Teach for America, Relay Graduate School, and charter school networks: the making of a parallel education structure. *Education Policy Analysis Archives, 24*(17 Teach For America: Research on Politics, Leadership, Race, and Education Reform), 1-30. doi:http://dx.doi.org/10.14507/epaa.24.2037

Mungal, A. S. (2015). Hybridized teacher education programs in NYC: A missed opportunity? *Education Policy Analysis Archives, 23* (New Public Management and the New Professionalism in Education: Compliance, Appropriation and Resistance), 1-32.

Mungal, A. S. (2012). *Competition or Partnerships? Faculty perceptions of alternative and professionalized teacher preparation programs.* Ann Arbor, MI: UMI Dissertation Publishing.

National Association of Elementary School Principals. (2018). *The principal's guide to building culturally responsive schools.* Retrieved July 10, 2019, from Alexandria, VA: https://www.naesp.org/sites/default/files/NAESP_Culturally_Responsive_Schools_Guide.pdf

National Association of Secondary School Principals. (2019). *Culturally responsive schools.* Retrieved July 21, 2019, from https://www.nassp.org/policy-advocacy-center/nassp-position-statements/culturally-responsive-schools/

National School Public Relations Association. (n.d.). *A principal's top 10 list for successful communications.* Retrieved July 23, 2019, from https://www.nspra.org/files/PrincipalsTop10.pdf

National Threat Assessment Center. (2018). *Enhancing school safety using a threat assessment model: An operational guide for preventing targeted school violence.* Washington, DC: U.S. Department of Homeland Security Retrieved July 21, 2019, from https://www.dhs.gov/sites/default/files/publications/18_0711_USSS_NTAC-Enhancing-School-Safety-Guide.pdf

National Voices for Equality Education and Enlightenment. (2019). Statistics. Retrieved July 15, 2019, from https://www.nveee.org/statistics/

New York State Education Department. (2016). *Addressing bullying, harassment, intimidation, and discrimination in our schools.* Retrieved July 23, 2019, from http://www.p12.nysed.gov/dignityact/documents/PreventBullyingInYourSchool_Nov2016.pdf

Nittle, N. K. (2019). How racism affects minority students in public schools. *Issues.* Retrieved July 14, 2019, from https://www.thoughtco.com/how-racism-affects-public-school-minorities-4025361

Northouse, P. G. (2017). *Introduction to leadership: Concepts and practice.* Thousand Oaks, CA: Sage.

Online Library of Liberty. (2019). *Lord Acton writes to Bishop Creighton.* Liberty Fund, Inc. Retrieved July 6, 2019, from https://oll.libertyfund.org/quotes/214

Oxford Reference. (2016). *Oxford essential quotations (4 ed.) – Helmuth von Moltke.* S. Ratcliffe, editor. Retrieved June 10, 2019, from https://www.oxfordreference.com/view/10.1093/acref/9780191826719.001.0001/q-oro-ed4-00007547

Ozono, H., Watabe, M., Yoshikawa, S., Nakashima, S., Rule, N., Ambady, N., & Adams, R. B. (2010). What's in a smile? Cultural differences in the effects of smiling on judgments of trustworthiness. *Letters on Evolutionary Behavioral Science, 1*(1), 15-18.

Pasqualis, L. (2017). *11 top responsibilities and 10 common mistakes of a technical leader.* Retrieved February 10, 2019, from https://www.coderhood.com/11-top-responsibilities-and-10-common-mistakes-of-a-technical-leader/

Perez-Isiah, R. (2018). The myth of colorblind. *Identity, Education and Power.* Retrieved from https://medium.com/identity-education-and-power/the-myth-of-colorblindness-9ee6604766d1

Porter, J. (2017). Why you should make time for self-reflection (Even if you hate doing it). *Managing Yourself.* Retrieved July 10, 2019, from https://hbr.org/2017/03/why-you-should-make-time-for-self-reflection-even-if-you-hate-doing-it

Project Implicit. (2011). Preliminary information. Retrieved July 21, 2019, from https://implicit.harvard.edu/implicit/takeatest.html

stopbullying.gov. (2019). *Prevention: Teach kids how to identify bullying and how to stand up to it safely.* Retrieved July 10, 2019, from https://www.stopbullying.gov

Psychology Today. (2019). Mindfulness. Retrieved July 21, 2019, from https://www.psychologytoday.com/us/basics/mindfulness

Rasmussen, R. K. (1998). *The quotable Mark Twain.* New York, NY: McGraw-Hill.

Reyna, A. M. (2017). *With great power comes great responsibility: Navigating year one of the principalship.* The University of Texas at El Paso: Proquest.

re:Work. (2019). *Unbiasing.* Retrieved July 21, 2019, from https://rework.withgoogle.com/subjects/unbiasing/

Rigsbee, C. (2009). What makes a principal great? Retrieved July 23, 2019, from https://www.edweek.org/tm/articles/2009/02/18/021109tln_rigsbee.h20.html

Rise. (2018). *Why workplace humour is the secret to great leadership.* Retrieved July 20, 2019, from https://risepeople.com/blog/why-workplace-humour-is-the-secret-to-great-leadership/

Robbins, S. P., & Judge, T. A. (2018). *Organizational behavior: Concepts, controversies, and applications.* Boston, MA: Pearson Education, Inc.

Roberts, B. W. (2016). *Can you change your personality traits?* Retrieved May 20, 2019, from https://www.div12.org/can-you-change-your-personality-traits/

Romero, E. J., & Cruthirds, K. W. (2006). The use of humor in the workplace. *Academy of Management Perspectives 20*(2), 58-69.

Sala, F. (2003). *Laughing all the way to the bank.* Retrieved July 23, 2019, from https://hbr.org/2003/09/laughing-all-the-way-to-the-bank

Selig, M. (2016). *The 9 superpowers of your smile.* Retrieved February 10, 2019, from https://www.psychologytoday.com/us/blog/changepower/201605/the-9-superpowers-your-smile

Shaw, P. L. (2012). *Taking charge: Leading with passion and purpose in the principalship.* New York, NY: Teachers College Press.

Sorenson, R. D., & Goldsmith, L. M. (2018). *The principal's guide to school budgeting.* Thousand Oaks, CA: Corwin.

Sorenson, R. D., Goldsmith, L. M., & DeMatthews, D. E. (2016). *The principal's guide to time management: Instructional leadership in the digital age.* Thousand Oaks, CA: Corwin.

Sorenson, R. D., & Goldsmith, L. M. (2009). *The principal's guide to managing school personnel*. Thousand Oaks, CA: Corwin.

Sorenson, R. D., Goldsmith, L. M., Méndez, Z. Y., & Maxwell, K. T. (2011). *The principal's guide to curriculum leadership*. Thousand Oaks, CA: Corwin.

Sorenson, R. D., & Mungal, A. S. (2019). *Field work: A voices of expertise – The instructional perspective of a successful school administrator*. Unpublished interview and conversation, Department of Educational Leadership and Foundations, The University of Texas at El Paso, El Paso, TX.

Sorenson, R. P. (2018). *Involved service: Healthcare or educational leadership? A son-to-father conversation*. Unpublished interview and conversation, Department of Educational Leadership and Foundations, The University of Texas at El Paso, El Paso, TX.

Southern Regional Education Board (SREB). (2019). *About SREB*. Retrieved July 21, 2019, from https://www.sreb.org/about

Staats, C. (2015). Understanding implicit bias: What educators should know. *American Educator*, Winter, 29-43.

Suttie, J. (2016). Fours ways teachers can reduce implicit bias. *Greater Good Magazine* Retrieved July 22, 2019, from https://greatergood.berkeley.edu/article/item/four_ways_teachers_can_reduce_implicit_bias

TeachThought Staff. (2019). *25 of the best resources for teaching critical thinking*. Retrieved July 12, 2019, from https://www.teachthought.com/critical-thinking/25-resources-for-teaching-critical-thinking/

The Teaching Alliance. (2019). *Culturally responsive teaching*. Retrieved July 10, 2019, from https://www.brown.edu/academics/education-alliance/teaching-diverse-learners/strategies-0/culturally-responsive-teaching-0

Thompson, E. (2019). *Understanding bullying and the necessity for prevention and intervention in school*. (Master's Senior Honors Thesis), Liberty University, Lynchberg, VA. Retrieved July 10, 2019, from https://digitalcommons.liberty.edu/cgi/viewcontent.cgi?article=1948&context=honors

Thompson, S. (2018). 5 steps to reduce unconscious bias in the workplace. *Blog*. Retrieved from https://www.lawsociety.org.uk/news/blog/5-steps-to-reduce-unconscious-bias-in-your-workplace/

U.S. Department of Education Office for Civil Rights. (2014). *Civil rights data collection data snapshot: School discipline*. Retrieved July 11, 2019, from Washington, DC: https://ocrdata.ed.gov/Downloads/CRDC-School-Discipline-Snapshot.pdf

U. S. Department of Homeland Security. (2019). *School safety and security*. Retrieved from https://www.dhs.gov/cisa/school-safety-and/security

Vitelli, R. (2015). *Can you change your personality?* Retrieved February 10, 2019, from https://www.psychologytoday.com/us/blog/media-spotlight/201509/can-you-change-your-personality

Weick, K. E., & Sutcliffe, K. M. (2001). *Managing the unexpected: Assuring high performance in an age of complexity* (1st ed.). San Francisco: Jossey-Bass.

Whitaker, T. (2012). *What great principals do differently: 18 things that matter most*. New York, NY: Routledge.

Yukl, G. A., & Gardner, III, W. L. (2019). *Leadership in organizations*. Boston, MA: Pearson Education, Inc.

Index

academic coaches: action or improvement plan development of, 59; principals learning and dependence on, 58–60, 64; professional development assistance of, 59; qualities of, 58–59; reflective learning and, 59; teacher and instructional capacity building of, 59; two-way communication establishment of, 59

ADA. *See* Americans with Disabilities Act

alternative and opposing views, 86; critique and critical thinking support in, 81; decision-making and problem-solving in, 81, 129; discussion question for, 87; good and bad news in, 80; leadership teams shared vision in, 81; outside-the-box thinking in, 81; school-site norms in, 80–81; student-focused in, 81; truth ignoring in, 80; understanding of, 80

Americans with Disabilities Act (ADA), 73

anticipation, case study on: application questions for, 68–69; "concerned citizens" and disgruntled stakeholders in, 67; district-wide community forum for plan in, 66–67; inappropriate adjustments in, 67–68; integration plan in, 66; principal adjusted response in, 67; principled leadership actions and, 68; racism and bigotry in, 66; school principal fortitude testing in, 66; students of color and poverty segregation in, 66; venting in, 67

Arlene Zarsky (fictional character), 17–19

Arnett Benson (fictional character), 17–19

Arnstein, S. R., 11

Bailey Quarters (fictional character), 107, 114

Batterson, Mark, 18

Baya, Vanessa (fictional character), 49–51

Bell Leadership Institute, 95

Bennett, N. A., 74

Benton C. Quest (fictional character): administrative report dislike of, 30; *eat the frog* preparation of, 31; student interaction love of, 31

Berra, Lawrence Peter "Yogi," 5, 7

bias, implicit: colorblindness rejection in, 75–76; culturally relevant pedagogy implementation

in, 76; culturally responsive pedagogy teacher strategies for, 76–77; culturally responsive schools information in, 77; data examination in, 74, 75; different culture promotion in, 76; disability in, 73; discussion questions on, 86; diverse community groups interaction for, 75; empathy increase for, 75; equity culture ensuring against, 76; gender identity and sexual orientation in, 73; individual aspects in, 72; institutional, 73; marginalized student story in, 73; naming or tackling of, 75; online questionnaires use in, 74; past biases and lack of awareness consideration in, 72; principal awareness of, 74; principals and school personnel practices influence of, 72; professional development and addressing of, 74–75, 85; racial and color and national origin discrimination in, 73; recruiting and selection practices review in, 74; religious discrimination in, 73; revise and revisit in, 76; school-related issues in, 72, 85; self-awareness increase for, 74–75; sex and gender in, 73; types of, 72, *73*; unconscious assumptions in, 72; understand impact of, 74; workplace bias elimination recommendations in, 74–76
Black Lives Matter, 126
Blackman, A., 74
Bosque Zavala (fictional character), 66–69
Brown, Alison, 62
Bublé, Michael, 89

capacity building, 3, 59; adaptation quality in, 104; authority delegation in, 110; Canadian geese allegory and application questions in, 114–16; car analogy #1 example in, 104; car analogy #2 in, 106; change environment creation in, 112; committee parameters in, 110; as continuous process, 112; deficiency unawareness in, 105; democratic ideals fostering in, 108; discussion questions on, 114; formal and informal observations rubrics creation in, 108; four stages of, 105–6; Hadden on, 108; individual or team accomplishment ability in, 104; instructional capacity fine-tuning processes for, 107–8; instructional foundation building in, 112; instructional work conversations in, 109; issues and circumstances interfering with, 103; leading and learning impact on, 103; learning community organization in, 113; life and career thinking in, 111; meditation and reflection time in, 110–11; mentoring in, 110; personal and professional refinement in, 106; principal statements about, 104–5; problem identification in, 112; problem-solving in, 112; professional areas consciousness in, 105–6; reflective conversations and instructional coaching in, 108; reflective practice in, 103–4; related terms to, 104; school constructs integration in, 112; school-site level incorporation of, 111–12; skills and expertise improvement in, 104; solid relationship development in, 109–10; student progress tech-tool incorporation in, 109, 113; student success and, 105; suggestions and criticism acceptance in, 110; sustainability strategies for, 112–13; taking action in, 106; teacher development support in, 105; teacher evaluation and professional development alignment in, 108–9;

teacher incompetence in, 106–7; thinking and stating and doing factors in, 103; top 11 tools for, 108–11, 113; why and how understanding in, 105–6
Castro, V., 74
Catherine Tomsky (fictional character), 8–9
Center for Teaching and Learning, 44
Chaplin, Charlie, 95
Chavez, Cesar, 71
Civil Rights Movement, 126
Coffin, William Sloane, 82
Columbine High School, 60
communication, 3, 28, 45, 59, 62–64, 91–94, 126; availability in, 79; customer service in, 78; discussion questions on, 86–87; early and often in, 77, 86; face-to-face, 77, 86; honesty and maintaining of, 78; learning community members relationship development in, 77; parental involvement in, 78; personal greetings consistency in, 78; plan development for, 78; short and simple messages in, 78; staff as ambassadors for, 78; superintendent story and questions regarding, 79–80
Connolly, M., 68
critical thinking, 4, 81; benefits of, 127; discussion question on, 131; important resource for, 127; Internet information navigation and, 127; student skills development in, 127; teacher professional development in, 127
Curphy, G. J., 41
cyberbullying, 3; anti-bully agenda reinforcement in, 124; case study and application questions on, 131–33; conduct and behavior policies for, 124; counselor support for, 124; discussion question on, 130; government website on, 123; health conditions caused by, 123; New York State Education Department information on, 123–24; parent decision-making inclusion and monitoring in, 124; professional development and resources for, 124; stakeholder guidelines development in, 124; zero-tolerance in, 124

Dalberg-Acton, John, 117
Day, O'Reilly (fictional character), 49–51
DeMatthews, D. E., 23, 108
Department of Homeland Security (DHS), 61–62, 64
Department of Justice, U. S., 72
DHS. *See* Department of Homeland Security

Eat the frog!, 30–32
Eckert, Jonathan, 103, 114
Eisenhower, Dwight D., 89, 95
equality and equity, 76; differences between, 122; discussion question on, 130; educational inequities in, 121; marginalized students and, 121; meritocracy and, 122; minority students facts about, 121; principal recognition of, 129; racial discrimination eradication aim of, 122; suspension rates in, 121; United States Declaration of Independence and, 121–22

Facebook, 123
Fiarman, S. E., 74, 75
Fitzgerald, Ella, 89
formal networks. *See* informal and formal networks
Franklin, Benjamin, 26
Fullan, M., 110

Gardner, W. L., III, 41
Ginnett, R. C., 41
Glasser's Reality Therapy, 83, 87–88
Goldsmith, L. M., 23, 108

Gone with the Wind (Mitchell), 120
Google Docs, 109
Google re:Work, 74

Hadden, K., 108
Hall, Pete, 103, 105
highly reliable organizations (HROs), 55–56
Hughes, R. L., 41
humor, 3; concluding chuckle in, 98; creativity and problem solving in, 96; daily use of, 96; discussion questions on, 99; distasteful and inappropriate, 96; goal clarity in, 96; Good Humor Man and Woman as neighborhood staple in, 94–95; good joke example in, 96–97; as highly effective leader habit, 97; human side of, 97, 98; laugh at self in, 96; leader competency in, 95–96; as leadership toolkit part, 95, 97; reaction prediction in, 96; research literature about, 95; stress diffusing with, 95; Twain and Chaplin on, 95; when and where incorporation of, 97

implicit bias. *See* bias, implicit
In a Pit with a Lion on a Snowy Day (Batterson), 18
informal and formal networks, 130; colleague relationship building in, 125; current issue insight in, 126; discussion question on, 131; family and friends support in, 126; isolation removal in, 125; leadership forming of, 45; mentorship and, 125; new principals aid in, 125; official approach in, 125; peer communication in, 126; as support system, 125
"inspect what you expect," 48, 58, 64
Instagram, 123
involved service: change recognition in, 12; common query in, 12; community elements in, 13; concept of, 11; data use in, 14; discovery in, 12; factors resulting from, 14–15, 17; form of, 11; healthcare industry root of, 11; instructional leadership incorporation in, 14; instructional program development in, 15; leader philosophy elements in, 13; open school culture and positive environment in, 14–15; participation and engagement in, 11; professional development leading in, 15; relationships and, 15; school elements in, 13; status quo change question and answer in, 12; student engagement in, 15; 10-essential elements in, 13–14, 17; traditional leadership and instructionally-oriented change in, 12; vision establishment in, 14
involved service, case study of: application questions for, 19–20; educationally-oriented lion chasing in, 19; leadership lesson in, 18–19; lion chaser story in, 18–19; old principal role description in, 17; participation and engagement in, 19; principal role change in, 18; reflection in, 18

Kleiser, Grenville, 89, 95

A Ladder of Participation (Arnstein), 11
law enforcement agents, 61; black student arrest rates in, 62; civil rights and student groups in, 62; news reports and, 62; principal communication with, 62–63; scrutiny increase in, 62; students and arrest and referral statistics in, 62, *65*; tension escalation and, 62; two perspectives on engagement of, 62
leadership, 5, 8, 27–28; active participation encouragement in, 39; authoritarian style of, 38, 39, 47; books and websites for,

Index 147

37; collaborative team spirit and unity creation in, 46; colleague consulting in, 45; continuity in, 42–43; current knowledge use in, 41; delegation and dumping fine line in, 44; delegation as mentoring in, 43, 48; democratic style of, 38, 39, 47; demographic change support in, 128–29; different styles incorporation in, 37; discussion questions for, 48; experienced teacher population burnouit in, 42; faculty and staff listening in, 39, 40; faculty consideration in, 39; faculty leadership and commitment change handling in, 43, 47–48; high achievers and at-risk students mentoring in, 44; humor as toolkit part in, 95, 97; informal and formal networks forming in, 45; information gathering critical in, 45; instructional style of, 38, 47; involved service and, 12, 14, 18–19; laissez-faire style of, 38, 47; leadership team and staff trust in, 45; multiple groups handling in, 38; new and experienced faculty investment and involvement in, 41–42, 47; new instructionally-focused initiatives steps in, 40; new teacher or staff support in, 41, 47; novice faculty perspectives in, 40; organization and, 26, 29–31; personnel and climate and culture understanding in, 46; principals and, 2, 16, 58, 63–64, 68; right people in right positions in, 44; self-reflection and communication in, 45; service style of, 38, 39, 47; shared responsibilities in, 39, 47; situational style of, 38, 47; student engagement and service-learning impact in, 44; student mentoring and support in, 44, 48; student teacher and principal interaction research in, 40–41, 47; student teacher feedback importance in, 41; style adaptation in, 38–39; styles of, *38*; superintendent advice on, 51; team visibility in, 55; transactional style of, 38, 47; transformational style of, 38, 47; "trust but verify" as navigational tool in, 47–48, 58; visibility as motivator in, 46; visionary style of, 38, 39, 47

leadership, case study on: application questions for, 50–51; assistant principal and volunteer interaction in, 49–50; campus-related projects in, 49; principal and situations handling in, 49–50; volunteer personalities in, 49

leadership skills (responsibilities), 9, 17; affirmation in, 10; challenge embracing in, 10–11; culture as, 10; discipline in, 10; focus and involvement in, 10; relationships and, 10; research literature and, 10; social judgment and perceptiveness in, 10; visibility as, 10

leadership team, 45, 63–64, 81

Leo Marvin (fictional character), 8–9

Les Nessman (fictional character), 106–8, 114

Linton, 75

Lopez, George, 95

marginalized groups, 73, 76–77, 85–86, 121

Marjory Stoneman Douglas High School, 60

Marzano, R. J., 10, 17

McEwan, E. K., 84, 87–88

McNulty, B. A., 10, 17

McQuerrey, L., 91, 99

mentoring, 28, 43–44, 48, 110, 125

Me Too Movement, 126

Microsoft e-Lesson on Unconscious Bias, 74

mindfulness: discussion question on, 65; early signals heeding in, 55; expertise deference in, 56;

failure preoccupation in, 56; HROs resiliency in, 55; interpretations simplification reluctance in, 56; key characteristics of, 55, *56*; operations sensitivity in, 56; proactive responding in, 55; resilience commitment in, 56; stress and anxiety reduction in, 55; unexpected events adjusting in, 55
Mitchell, Margaret, 120
Mohan, Rudy (fictional character), 49–51
Moltke, Helmuth van, 53
Morrison, Ann, 71

Nader, Ralph, 37
NAESP. *See* National Association of Elementary School Principals
NASSP. *See* National Association of Secondary School Principals
National Association of Elementary School Principals (NAESP), 77
National Association of Secondary School Principals (NASSP), 77
National School Public Relations Association, 77
new principal academy, 16; academy presenter question in, 6; leadership development in, 5; obstacles understanding in, 6; personal and professional journeys in, 6; role embracing in, 6
New York State Education Department, 123–24

Occupy Wall Street (OWS), 126
organization: benefits of, 22–25; collaboration and planning improvement in, 23; daily leadership practices for, 26; discussion questions for, 32–33; *Eat the frog!* quote in, 30; Franklin on, 26; leadership behavior assessment and scoring instructions for, 29–30; methodical and systematical approach to, 22; obsolete and unneeded items reduction in, 24; open and accessible workspace in, 24; parents and volunteers use in, 23; productivity increase in, 22; promotion possibilities in, 24; questions about, 21–22; Quest's leadership model for, 30–31; relationships improvement in, 24–25; reputation enhancement in, 23; Rios case study and application questions about, 33–35; self-esteem and confidence increase in, 24; social studies teacher story about, 21; stress reduction in, 22; success and failure correlation with, 21; time management in, 22–23; top-10 daily habits and routines for, 25. *See also* preparation
OWS. *See* Occupy Wall Street

people skills assessment test: directions for, 99; scoring interpretations for, 100–101; statements for, 100
Perez-Isiah, R., 74
PLC. *See* professional learning community
preparation, 21; communication regularity in, 28; complexity management in, 28; creativity and innovation fostering in, 28; discussion questions for, 32–33; *Eat the frog!* quote in, 30; follower-leader dynamics in, 28; future vision development in, 28; ineffective personality attributes in, *28*; leadership behavior assessment and scoring instructions for, 29–30; leadership preparedness skills and traits in, 27–28; mentorship in, 28; positive and appropriate traits in, 28; Quest's leadership model for, 30–31; relationships creation in, 28; research-based skill sets in, 26–27; Rios case study and application

questions about, 33–35; 7 Bs of preparedness in, 27

principals, 18, 49–50, 74, 125, 127; academic coaches and, 58–60, 64; adaptability of, 64; adjustments allowing of, 69; alternative views encouragement of, 80–81; anticipation case study and, 66–67; anxiety in, 5; capacity building of, 3, 104–5; casual and conversational interaction with, 54; collective leadership and, 16; communication and, 3, 62–64, 77–79; concerns value and addressing of, 82; core preparation skills of, 32; crisis prevention of, 64; daily organization of, 31–32; demographic change support of, 128–29; demographics knowledge of, 80; desk resource of, 1–2; destiny influencing of, 5; discussion questions in, 16–17, 65; diversity embracing of, 3, 82–83, 86; "do-it-now" mentality of, 2, 32; *eat the frog* concept and, 32; ego and confidence levels of, 118, 129; focus of, 1; "fork in the road" and, 7; good humor incorporation of, 3; great ideas sharing of, 1; image projection interpretation and understanding of, 117–18, 129; "inspect what you expect" as, 48, 58, 64; as involved servants, 2; journeys of, 16; law enforcement agents engagement and, 62–63; leadership and instructional team norms establishment of, 58; leadership team reliance of, 63–64; long- and short-term planning of, 53; marginalized groups and, 76–77, 85–86, 121; meeting availability of, 82; mindfulness and, 55–56; Monday morning meeting of, 54; never say "no" and, 82; own self-interest story of, 117; personal time establishment of, 53; positive self-concept and attitude maintaining of, 32; positive site-level differences of, 7; pot-hole avoidance in, 6; previous week events reflection of, 54; principled leadership actions of, 68; procedure change discussion in, 54; reasons for becoming, 71–72; reflection and, 16; reputation desire of, 7; school personnel administrative schedule awareness of, 118; school personnel as "eyes and ears" of, 63; self-reflection of, 3; serious considerations of, 6; similar events and different outcomes handling of, 63–64; situational and shared leadership of, 2; SMART goals and, 58, 64; social media and, 3; specialized knowledge gain in, 1; stakeholder connecting of, 82; as strangers, 90; student mindfulness of, 65; student teacher interaction with, 40–41, 47; successful indicators for, 7, 17; top-down demands on, 63; transformational-leverage leadership and, 16; "trust but verify" as, 47–48, 58, 64, 110; unexpected events adjusting of, 55; upcoming events anticipation of, 54; visible presence and use of, 54, 64, 81–82, 118; as visionary leaders, 1; work week anticipation of, 2

principals, people-centered, 98; assertiveness and confidence sustaining in, 93–94; barrier decoding of, 92; charm and, 94; conflict management and, 93; daily meeting and greeting of, 90; discussion questions on, 99; faculty meeting vignette about, 92–93; good people skills definition in, 91; interpersonal communication skills importance in, 91, 94; listen and hear and understand in, 91; non-verbal communication recognizing of, 92–93; people needs and points of view understanding of, 93; people skills assessment test for, 99–101; as perceptive and intuitive, 94; personal integrity and statements in, 93; personality traits changing in, 91; rapport building of, 94; respecting and managing differences as, 93; strong communication skills as, 94; student interaction and knowledge of, 90

The Principal's Guide to Time Management (Sorenson and Goldsmith and DeMatthews), 23, 108

problem-solving: alternative and opposing views in, 81, 129; capacity building and, 112; conflict and, 120; difference bridging in, 120; follow-up in, 120; forward thinking in, 120; humor and creativity in, 96; new day and new opportunities in, 120; old problems in, 120; oppositional views handling in, 120–21; pros and cons weighing in, 120; "tomorrow is another day" notion in, 121

professional development, 15, 108–9, 123–24, 127–28; academic coaches assistance in, 59; bias addressing in, 74–75, 85

professional learning community (PLC), 59, 77, 113, 127

Project Implicit, 74

Raj, Molly (fictional character), 49–51

relationships, 10, 15, 24–25, 28, 77, 109–10, 125

Relay Graduate School, 128

Reyna, Angela, 45, 125

Rios, Sandra (fictional character), 33–35

Robert Wiley School: faculty and staff stress at, 8–9; leadership lack at, 8; Marvin primary purpose at, 8; reflection questions about, 9; school secretary embezzlement scheme at, 8; Tomsky's state-mandated instructional initiative concern in, 8

Sandy Hook Elementary School, 60

school security: DHS threat assessment process in, 61; fire-drills and, 60; new rule look in, *60*; principal vigilance and, 60; school response change in, 60; Targeted Violence Prevention Plan steps for, 61; unsettling local events and, 60; violent attacks and, 60

self-reflection, 3, 16, 18, 118, 120, 129; capacity building and, 103–4, 108, 110–11; discussion question on, 130; forms of, 119; insights and solutions in, 119; leadership and, 45; personal actions or inactions meaning making in, 119; previous week events in, 54; questions for, 119; specific issue focus in, 119

Simeral, Alisa, 103

Singleton, 75

SMART. *See* specific, measurable, achievable, realistic, and time-bound goals

smile: brain's anterior temporal region beginning of, 89; discussion question on, 98; positive start with, 90, 98; response to, 89; ten unique things about, 89–90

social movements, 3; principal and learning community awareness in, 127; social consciousness changing in, 126; student social inequities awareness in, 126; world events connections in, 126

social networking and social media, 3; apps and websites in, 122; discussion question on, 130; first adapters to, 123; new apps in, 123; power and problems in, 123; professional development for, 123; school policies for, 123; special interests and, 123; student participation increase with, 122; as useful tool, 122

Sorenson, R. D., 23, 108

specific, measurable, achievable, realistic, and time-bound (*SMART*) goals, 58, 65
students, 15, 31, 65, 66, 90, 122, 126; alternative and opposing views and, 81; arrest and referral statistics of, 62, *65*; capacity building and, 105, 109, 113; critical thinking skills development of, 127; difficult teachers impact on, 83–84; leadership and, 44, 48; marginalized, 73, 121
Sutcliffe, K. M., 55
Suttie, J., 74

Targeted Violence Prevention Plan: behaviors defining in, 61; central reporting system creation and training in, 61; discussion question on, 65; law enforcement intervention threshold determination in, 61; multidisciplinary threat assessment team establishment in, 61; risk management options development in, 61; safe school climate promotion in, 61; threat assessment procedures creation for, 61
teachers, 21; academic coaches instructional capacity building of, 59; alternative preparation programs and, 128; capacity building and, 105–9; critical thinking professional development for, 127; culturally responsive pedagogy strategies for, 76–77; leadership and, 40–42, 47; learning styles professional development for, 128
teachers, difficult: case study application and questions on, 87–88; discussion question on, 87; as dissenters, 84; engagement and support of, 84; Glasser's Reality Therapy aid use in, 83, 87–88; immediate attention and action in, 85; inappropriate actions documenting of, 85; issues with, 83; negative impact limiting of, 85; as positive influences, 84; recommendations for working with, 84; situation addressing of, 83; strengths and interests focus on, 84; student gravitation toward, 84; student negative impact of, 83; transparency in, 83, 86; trust establishment with, 83; valued and being heard in, 83–84
Teach For America, 128
Teachthought, 127
Thompson, S., 74
"trust but verify," 47–48, 58, 64, 110
Twain, Mark, 30, 95
Twitter, 123

unexpected event management, 55; discussion questions on, 65; error-friendly environment in, 57; honesty in, 57–58; humility cultivation in, 57; school culture and, 57; school goals in, 57; skeptic support in, 57; three categories of, 56–57; uncertainty welcoming in, 58; values balance preservation in, 57; vulnerability awareness in, 57
University of Missouri, Kansas City, 89–90

Van Velsor, Ellen, 71
visibility, 10, 46, 54–55, 64, 81–82, 118

Waters, T., 10, 17
Weick, K. E., 55
"When You're Smiling," 89
White, Randall, 71
Williams, Robin, 95
With Great Power Comes Great Responsibility (Reyna), 45
Wolf, Michelle, 95
Women's Rights Movement, 126
Working Together (Eckert), 114

Yukl, G. A., 41

About the Authors

Dr. Angus S. Mungal is a faculty member in the Educational Leadership and Foundations Department at The University of Texas at El Paso where he teaches in the doctoral program and the K–12 leadership program. He teaches doctoral level courses in Qualitative Research, Evaluation, Accountability and Policy Analysis, Leadership and Advocacy in Education, and the Introduction to Doctoral Studies. He also teaches a K–12 principal preparation course, Educational Leadership in a Diverse Society, as well as a superintendent preparation course, Educational Policy Development.

Dr. Mungal earned his doctorate at New York University. He worked for three years in Kanagawa-ken in Japan. He is originally from Trinidad and Tobago in the Caribbean, and grew up in Toronto, Canada.

Dr. Mungal has published in numerous policy and education journals. His focuses are on education policy and community. Specifically, he has written on alternative teacher and leadership routes; the impact of marketization on education; critical discourse analysis; afterschool policies; marginalized groups; culturally relevant pedagogies; institutionalized bias; student teachers; school leadership; and the principalship.

Dr. Mungal has also published with his co-author, Dr. Richard Sorenson, in practitioner journals. He is most proud of the work he has done with his doctoral students, including publications on women in academia and the glass ceiling, and various manuscripts on military students transitioning into higher education. He continues to encourage his students to publish.

Dr. Richard Sorenson resides in El Paso, Texas, on the U.S. Mexico border, in a home that faces the majestic Franklin Mountains. Dr. Sorenson, professor emeritus, is the former director of the Principal Preparation Program and chairperson of the Educational Leadership and Foundations Department at

The University of Texas at El Paso (UTEP). He earned his doctorate from Texas A&M University at Corpus Christi. He served for 25 years as a social studies teacher, assistant principal, principal, and associate superintendent for human resources.

Dr. Sorenson works with graduate students at UTEP in the areas of school-based budgeting, personnel, educational law, and leadership development. He has previously been named The University of Texas at El Paso College of Education Professor of the Year, and he is an active writer with numerous professional journal publications.

Dr. Sorenson has also authored seven principal leadership textbooks, as well as teacher resource guides and student workbooks. He has been actively involved in numerous professional organizations, including the Texas Elementary Principals and Supervisors Association (TEPSA) and the Texas Association of Secondary School Principals (TASSP), for which he conducted annual new-principal academy seminars.

Dr. Sorenson has been married to his best friend and wife, Donna, for the past 43 years and has two adult children, Lisa and Ryan, a wonderful son-in-law, Sam, and three young grandchildren, Savannah, Nehemiah, and Amelia—all of whom are the pride and joy of his life.

www.ingramcontent.com/pod-product-compliance
Lightning Source LLC
Chambersburg PA
CBHW020741230426
43665CB00009B/512